THE BURGESS BIRD BOOK FOR CHILDREN

ALSO AVAILABLE FROM LIVING BOOK PRESS

The Burgess Animal Book for Children (in color)

Home Geography
Elementary Geography
Viking Tales
Parables From Nature*
Fifty Famous Stories Retold*
The Blue Fairy Book*
        * in AO reading order

Richard Halliburton's Marvels of the Orient
Richard Halliburton's Marvels of the Occident

Charlotte Mason's Home Education Series

1. Home Education
2. Parents and Children
3. School Education
4. Ourselves
5. Formation of Character
6. A Philosophy of Education

And many, many more!

All Living Book Press titles are complete and unabridged, and presented with the original illustrations, sometimes from several sources, to bring these great books even more to life.

To see a complete list of all our releases or if you wish to leave us any feedback please visit www.livingbookpress.com

The Burgess Bird Book For Children

THORNTON BURGESS

ILLUSTRATED BY

LOUIS AGASSIZ FUERTES

This edition published 2018
by Living Book Press

Original edition published in 1919.

ISBN: 978-1-925729-24-5 (paperback)
978-1-922348-28-9 (hardback)
978-1-922348-58-6 (black and white paperback)

A catalogue record for this
book is available from the
National Library of Australia

Contents

	Preface	vii
i.	Jenny Wren Arrives.	1
ii.	The Old Orchard Bully.	6
iii.	Jenny Has a Good Word for Some Sparrows.	10
iv.	Chippy, Sweetvoice, and Dotty.	14
v.	Peter Learns Something He Hadn't Guessed.	21
vi.	An Old Friend In a New Home.	27
vii.	The Watchman of the Old Orchard.	33
viii.	Old Clothes and Old Houses.	39
ix.	Longbill and Teeter.	43
x.	Redwing and Yellow Wing.	49
xi.	Drummers and Carpenters.	56
xii.	Some Unlikely Relatives.	62
xiii.	More of the Blackbird Family.	68
xiv.	Bob White and Carol the Meadow Lark.	74
xv.	A Swallow and One Who Isn't.	80
xvi.	A Robber in the Old Orchard.	87
xvii.	More Robbers.	91
xviii.	Some Homes in the Green Forest.	96
xix.	A Maker of Thunder and a Friend in Black.	102
xx.	A Fisherman Robbed.	108
xxi.	A Fishing Party.	114
xxii.	Some Feathered Diggers.	120
xxiii.	Some Big Mouths.	125
xxiv.	The Warblers Arrive.	129
xxv.	Three Cousins Quite Unlike.	135
xxvi.	Peter Gets a Lame Neck.	139
xxvii.	A New Friend and an Old One.	144
xxviii.	Peter Sees Rosebreast and Finds Redcoat.	150

XXIX.	The Constant Singers.	157
XXX.	Jenny Wren's Cousins.	161
XXXI.	Voices of the Dusk.	167
XXXII.	Peter Saves a Friend and Learns Something.	173
XXXIII.	A Royal Dresser and a Late Nester.	178
XXXIV.	Mourner the Dove and Cuckoo.	184
XXXV.	A Butcher and a Hummer.	190
XXXVI.	A Stranger and a Dandy.	196
XXXVII.	Farewells and Welcomes.	201
XXXVIII.	Honker and Dippy Arrive.	207
XXXIX.	Peter Discovers Two Old Friends.	212
XL.	Some Merry Seed-Eaters.	216
XLI.	More Friends Come With the Snow.	221
XLII.	Peter Learns Something About Spooky.	225
XLIII.	Queer Feet and a Queerer Bill.	230
XLIV.	More Folks in Red.	234
XLV.	Peter Sees Two Terrible Feathered Hunters.	239

PREFACE

THIS BOOK was written to supply a definite need. Its preparation was undertaken at the urgent request of booksellers and others who have felt the lack of a satisfactory medium of introduction to bird life for little children. As such, and in no sense whatever as a competitor with the many excellent books on this subject, but rather to supplement these, this volume has been written.

Its primary purpose is to interest the little child in, and to make him acquainted with, those feathered friends he is most likely to see. Because there is no method of approach to the child mind equal to the story, this method of conveying information has been adopted. So far as I am aware the book is unique in this respect. In its preparation an earnest effort has been made to present as far as possible the important facts regarding the appearance, habits and characteristics of our feathered neighbors. It is intended to be at once a story book and an authoritative handbook. While it is intended for little children, it is hoped that children of larger growth may find in it much of both interest and helpfulness.

Mr. Louis Agassiz Fuertes, artist and naturalist, has marvelously supplemented such value as may be in the text by his wonderful drawings in full color. They were made especially for this volume and are so accurate, so true to life, that study of them will enable any one to identify the species shown. I am greatly indebted to Mr. Fuertes for his cooperation in the endeavor to make this book of real assistance to the beginner in the study of our native birds.

It is offered to the reader without apologies of any sort. It was written as a labor of love—love for little children and love for the birds. If as a result of it even a few children are led to a keener interest in and better understanding of our feathered friends, its purpose will have been accomplished.

THORNTON W. BURGESS

I. Jenny Wren Arrives.

Lipperty-lipperty-lip scampered Peter Rabbit behind the tumble-down stone wall along one side of the Old Orchard. It was early in the morning, very early in the morning. In fact, jolly, bright Mr. Sun had hardly begun his daily climb up in the blue, blue sky. It was nothing unusual for Peter to see jolly Mr. Sun get up in the morning. It would be more unusual for Peter not to see him, for you know Peter is a great hand to stay out all night and not go back to the dear Old Briar-patch, where his home is, until the hour when most folks are just getting out of bed.

Peter had been out all night this time, but he wasn't sleepy, not the least teeny, weeny bit. You see, sweet Mistress Spring had arrived, and there was so much happening on every side, and Peter was so afraid he would miss something, that he wouldn't have slept at all if he could have helped it. Peter had come over to the Old Orchard so early this morning to see if there had been any new arrivals the day before.

"Birds are funny creatures," said Peter, as he hopped over a low place in the old stone wall and was fairly in the Old Orchard.

"Tut, tut, tut, tut, tut!" cried a rather sharp scolding voice. "Tut, tut, tut, tut, tut! You don't know what you are talking about, Peter Rabbit. They are not funny creatures at all. They are the most sensible folks in all the wide world."

Peter cut a long hop short right in the middle, to sit up with shining eyes. "Oh, Jenny Wren, I'm so glad to see you! When did you arrive?" he cried.

"Mr. Wren and I have just arrived, and thank goodness we are here at last," replied Jenny Wren, fussing about, as only she can, in a branch above Peter. "I never was more thankful in my life to see a place than I am right this minute to see the Old Orchard once more. It seems ages and ages since we left it."

"Well, if you are so fond of it what did you leave it for?" demanded Peter. "It is just as I said before—you birds are funny creatures. You never stay put; at least a lot of you don't. Sammy Jay and Tommy Tit the Chickadee and Drummer the Woodpecker and a few others have a little sense; they don't go off on long, foolish journeys. But the rest of you—"

"Tut, tut, tut, tut, tut!" interrupted Jenny Wren. "You don't know what you are talking about, and no one sounds so silly as one who tries to talk about something he knows nothing about."

Peter chuckled. "That tongue of yours is just as sharp as ever," said he. "But just the same it is good to hear it. We certainly would miss it. I was beginning to be a little worried for fear something might have happened to you so that you wouldn't be back here this summer. You know me well enough, Jenny Wren, to know that you can't hurt me with your tongue, sharp as it is, so you may as well save your breath to tell me a few things I want to know. Now if you are as fond of the Old Orchard as you pretend to be, why did you ever leave it?"

Jenny Wren's bright eyes snapped. "Why do you eat?" she asked tartly.

"Because I'm hungry," replied Peter promptly.

"What would you eat if there were nothing to eat?" snapped Jenny.

"That's a silly question," retorted Peter.

"No more silly than asking me why I leave the Old Orchard," replied Jenny. "Do give us birds credit for a little common sense, Peter. We can't live without eating any more than you can, and in winter there is no food at all here for most of us, so we go where there is food. Those who are lucky enough to eat the kinds of food that can be found here in winter stay here. They are lucky. That's what they are—lucky. Still—" Jenny Wren paused.

"Still what?" prompted Peter.

"I wonder sometimes if you folks who are at home all the time know just what a blessed place home is," replied Jenny. "It is only six months since we went south, but I said it seems ages, and it does. The best part of going away is coming home.

JENNY WREN. This is the saucy little House Wren who builds near your home.

BULLY THE ENGLISH SPARROW, the common sparrow of the streets.
CHIPPY THE CHIPPING SPARROW, the smallest of the family.

I don't care if that does sound rather mixed; it is true just the same. It isn't home down there in the sunny South, even if we do spend as much time there as we do here. *This* is home, and there's no place like it! What's that, Mr. Wren? I haven't seen all the Great World? Perhaps I haven't, but I've seen enough of it, let me tell you that! Anyone who travels a thousand miles twice a year as we do has a right to express an opinion, especially if they have used their eyes as I have mine. There is no place like home, and you needn't try to tease me by pretending that there is. My dear, I know you; you are just as tickled to be back here as I am."

"He sings as if he were," said Peter, for all the time Mr. Wren was singing with all his might.

Jenny Wren looked over at Mr. Wren fondly. "Isn't he a dear to sing to me like that? And isn't it a perfectly beautiful spring song?" said she. Then, without waiting for Peter to reply, her tongue rattled on. "I do wish he would be careful. Sometimes I am afraid he will overdo. Just look at him now! He is singing so hard that he is shaking all over. He always is that way. There is one thing true about us Wrens, and this is that when we do things we do them with all our might. When we work we work with all our might. When Mr. Wren sings he sings with all his might."

"And, when you scold you scold with all your might," interrupted Peter mischievously.

Jenny Wren opened her mouth for a sharp reply, but laughed instead. "I suppose I do scold a good deal," said she, "but if I didn't goodness knows who wouldn't impose on us. I can't bear to be imposed on."

"Did you have a pleasant journey up from the sunny South?" asked Peter.

"Fairly pleasant," replied Jenny. "We took it rather easily. Some birds hurry right through without stopping, but I should think they would be tired to death when they arrive. We rest whenever we are tired, and just follow along behind Mistress Spring, keeping far enough behind so that if she has to turn back we will not get caught by Jack Frost. It gives us time to get our new suits on the way. You know everybody expects you to have new things when you return home. How do you like my new suit, Peter?" Jenny bobbed and twisted and turned to show it off. It was plain to see that she was very proud of it.

"Very much," replied Peter. "I am very fond of brown. Brown and gray are my favorite colors." You know Peter's own coat is brown and gray.

"That is one of the most sensible things I have heard you say," chattered Jenny Wren. "The more I see of bright colors the better I like brown. It always is in good taste. It goes well with almost everything. It is neat and it is useful. If there is need of getting out of sight in a hurry you can do it if you wear brown. But if you wear bright colors it isn't so easy. I never envy anybody who happens to have brighter clothes than mine. I've seen dreadful things happen all because of wearing bright colors."

"What?" demanded Peter.

"I'd rather not talk about them," declared Jenny in a very emphatic way. "'Way down where we spent the winter some of the feathered folks who live there all the year round wear the brightest and most beautiful suits I've ever seen. They are simply gorgeous. But I've noticed that in times of danger these are the folks dreadful things happen to. You see they simply can't get out of sight. For my part I would far rather be simply and neatly dressed and feel safe than to wear wonderful clothes and never know a minute's peace. Why, there are some families I know of which, because of their beautiful suits, have been so hunted by men that hardly any are left. But gracious, Peter Rabbit, I can't sit here all day talking to you! I must find out who else has arrived in the Old Orchard and must look my old house over to see if it is fit to live in."

II. The Old Orchard Bully.

Peter Rabbit's eyes twinkled when Jenny Wren said that she must look her old house over to see if it was fit to live in. "I can save you that trouble," said he.

"What do you mean?" Jenny's voice was very sharp.

"Only that your old house is already occupied," replied Peter. "Bully the English Sparrow has been living in it for the last two months. In fact, he already has a good-sized family there."

"What?" screamed Jenny and Mr. Wren together. Then without even saying good-by to Peter, they flew in a great rage to see if he had told them the truth. Presently he heard them scolding as fast as their tongues could go, and this is very fast indeed.

"Much good that will do them," chuckled Peter. "They will have to find a new house this year. All the sharp tongues in the world couldn't budge Bully the English sparrow. My, my, my, my, just hear that racket! I think I'll go over and see what is going on."

So Peter hopped to a place where he could get a good view of Jenny Wren's old home and still not be too far from the safety of the old stone wall. Jenny Wren's old home had been in a hole in one of the old apple-trees. Looking over to it, Peter could see Mrs. Bully sitting in the little round doorway and quite filling it. She was shrieking excitedly. Hopping and flitting from twig to twig close by were Jenny and Mr. Wren, their tails pointing almost straight up to the sky, and scolding as fast as they could make their tongues go. Flying savagely at one and then at the other, and almost drowning their voices with his own harsh cries, was Bully himself. He was perhaps one fourth larger than Mr. Wren, although he looked half again as big. But for the fact that his new spring suit was very dirty, due to his fondness for taking dust baths and the fact that he cares nothing about his personal appearance and takes no care of himself, he would have been a fairly good-looking fellow. His back was more or less of an ashy color with black and chestnut stripes. His wings were brown with a white bar on each. His throat and breast were black, and below that he was of a dirty white. The sides of his throat were white and the back of his neck chestnut.

By ruffling up his feathers and raising his wings slightly as he hopped about, he managed to make himself appear much bigger than he really was. He looked like a regular little fighting savage. The noise had brought all the other birds in the Old Orchard to see what was going on, and every one of them was screaming and urging Jenny and Mr. Wren to stand up for their rights. Not one of them had a good word for Bully and his wife. It certainly was a disgraceful neighborhood squabble.

Bully the English Sparrow is a born fighter. He never is happier than when he is in the midst of a fight or a fuss of some kind. The fact that all his neighbors were against him didn't bother Bully in the least.

Jenny and Mr. Wren are no cowards, but the two together were no match for Bully. In fact, Bully did not hesitate to fly fiercely at any of the onlookers who came near enough, not even when they were twice his own size. They could have driven him from the Old Orchard had they set out to, but just by his boldness and appearance he made them afraid to try.

All the time Mrs. Bully sat in the little round doorway, encouraging him. She knew that as long as she sat there it would be impossible for either Jenny or Mr. Wren to get in. Truth to tell, she was enjoying it all, for she is as quarrelsome and as fond of fighting as is Bully himself.

"You're a sneak! You're a robber! That's my house, and the sooner you get out of it the better!" shrieked Jenny Wren, jerking her tail with every word as she hopped about just out of reach of Bully.

"It may have been your house once, but it is mine now, you little snip-of-nothing!" cried Bully, rushing at her like a little fury. "Just try to put us out if you dare! You didn't make this house in the first place, and you deserted it when you went south last fall. It's mine now, and there isn't anybody in the Old Orchard who can put me out."

Peter Rabbit nodded. "He's right there," muttered Peter. "I don't like him and never will, but it is true that he has a perfect right to that house. People who go off and leave things for half a year shouldn't expect to find them just as they left them. My, my, my what a dreadful noise! Why don't they all get together and drive Bully and Mrs. Bully out of the Old Orchard? If they don't I'm afraid he will drive them out. No one likes to live with such quarrelsome neighbors. They don't belong over in this country, anyway, and we would be a lot better off if they were not here. But I must say I do have to admire their spunk."

All the time Bully was darting savagely at this one and that one and having a thoroughly good time, which is more than could be said of any one else, except Mrs. Bully.

"I'll teach you folks to know that I am in the Old Orchard to stay!" shrieked Bully. "If you don't like it, why don't you fight? I am not afraid of any of you or all of you together." This was boasting, plain boasting, but it was effective. He actually made the other birds believe it. Not one of them dared stand up to him and fight. They were content to call him a bully and all the bad names they could think of, but that did nothing to help Jenny and Mr. Wren recover their house. Calling another bad names never hurts him. Brave deeds and not brave words are what count.

How long that disgraceful squabble in the Old Orchard would have lasted had it not been for something which happened, no one knows. Right in the midst of it some one discovered Black Pussy, the cat who lives in Farmer Brown's house, stealing up through the Old Orchard, her tail twitching and her yellow eyes glaring eagerly. She had heard that dreadful racket and suspected that in the midst of such excitement she might have a chance to catch one of the feathered folks. You can always trust Black Pussy to be on hand at a time like that.

No sooner was she discovered than everything else was forgotten. With Bully in the lead, and Jenny and Mr. Wren close behind him, all the birds turned their attention to Black Pussy.

She was the enemy of all, and they straightway forgot their own quarrel. Only Mrs. Bully remained where she was, in the little round doorway of her house. She intended to take no chances, but she added her voice to the general racket. How those birds did shriek and scream! They darted down almost into the face of Black Pussy, and none went nearer than Bully the English Sparrow and Jenny Wren.

Now Black Pussy hates to be the center of so much attention. She knew that, now she had been discovered, there wasn't a chance in the world for her to catch one of those Old Orchard folks. So, with tail still twitching angrily, she turned and, with such dignity as she could, left the Old Orchard. Clear to the edge of it the birds followed, shrieking, screaming, calling her bad names, and threatening to do all sorts of dreadful things to her, quite as if they really could.

When finally she disappeared towards Farmer Brown's barn, those angry voices changed. It was such a funny change that Peter Rabbit laughed right out. Instead of anger there was triumph in every note as everybody returned to attend to his own affairs. Jenny and Mr. Wren seemed to have forgotten all about Bully and his wife in their old house. They flew to another part of the Old Orchard, there to talk it all over and rest and get their breath. Peter Rabbit waited to see if they would not come over near enough to him for a little more gossip. But they didn't, and finally Peter started for his home in the dear Old Briar-patch. All the way there he chuckled as he thought of the spunky way in which Jenny and Mr. Wren had stood up for their rights.

III. Jenny Has a Good Word for Some Sparrows.

The morning after the fight between Jenny and Mr. Wren and Bully the English Sparrow found Peter Rabbit in the Old Orchard again. He was so curious to know what Jenny Wren would do for a house that nothing but some very great danger could have kept him away from there. Truth to tell, Peter was afraid that not being able to have their old house, Jenny and Mr. Wren would decide to leave the Old Orchard altogether. So it was with a great deal of relief that as he hopped over a low place in the old stone wall he heard Mr. Wren singing with all his might.

The song was coming from quite the other side of the Old Orchard from where Bully and Mrs. Bully had set up housekeeping. Peter hurried over. He found Mr. Wren right away, but at first saw nothing of Jenny. He was just about to ask after her when he caught sight of her with a tiny stick in her bill. She snapped her sharp little eyes at him, but for once her tongue was still. You see, she couldn't talk and carry that stick at the same time. Peter watched her and saw her disappear in a little hole in a big branch of one of the old apple-trees. Hardly had she popped in than she popped out again. This time her mouth was free, and so was her tongue.

"You'd better stop singing and help me," she said to Mr. Wren sharply. Mr. Wren obediently stopped singing and began to hunt for a tiny little twig such as Jenny had taken into that hole.

"Well!" exclaimed Peter. "It didn't take you long to find a new house, did it?"

"Certainly not," snapped Jenny "We can't afford to sit around wasting time like some folk I know."

Peter grinned and looked a little foolish, but he didn't resent it. You see he was quite used to that sort of thing. "Aren't you afraid that Bully will try to drive you out of that house?" he ventured.

Jenny Wren's sharp little eyes snapped more than ever. "I'd like to see him try!" said she. "That doorway's too small for him to get more than his head in. And if he tries putting his head in while I'm inside, I'll peck his eyes out!" She said this so fiercely that Peter laughed right out.

"I really believe you would," said he.

"I certainly would," she retorted. "Now I can't stop to talk to you, Peter Rabbit, because I'm too busy. Mr. Wren, you ought to know that that stick is too big." Jenny snatched it out of Mr. Wren's mouth and dropped it on the ground, while Mr. Wren meekly went to hunt for another. Jenny joined him, and as Peter watched them he understood why Jenny is so often spoken of as a feathered busybody.

For some time Peter Rabbit watched Jenny and Mr. Wren carry sticks and straws into that little hole until it seemed to him they were trying to fill the whole inside of the tree. Just watching them made Peter positively tired. Mr. Wren would stop every now and then to sing, but Jenny didn't waste a minute. In spite of that she managed to talk just the same.

"I suppose Little Friend the Song Sparrow got here some time ago," said she.

Peter nodded. "Yes," said he. "I saw him only a day or two ago over by the Laughing Brook, and although he wouldn't say so, I'm sure that he has a nest and eggs already."

Jenny Wren jerked her tail and nodded her head vigorously. "I suppose so," said she. "He doesn't have to make as long a journey as we do, so he gets here sooner. Did you ever in your life see such a difference as there is between Little Friend and his cousin, Bully? Everybody loves Little Friend."

Once more Peter nodded. "That's right," said he. "Everybody does love Little Friend. It makes me feel sort of all glad inside just to hear him sing. I guess it makes everybody feel that way. I wonder why we so seldom see him up here in the Old Orchard."

"Because he likes damp places with plenty of bushes better," replied Jenny Wren. "It wouldn't do for everybody to like the same kind of a place. He isn't a tree bird, anyway. He likes to be on or near the ground. You will never find his nest much above the ground, not more than a foot or two. Quite often it is on the ground. Of course I prefer Mr. Wren's song, but I must admit that Little Friend has one of the happiest songs of any one I know. Then, too, he is so modest, just like us Wrens."

Peter turned his head aside to hide a smile, for if there is anybody who delights in being both seen and heard it is Jenny Wren, while Little Friend the Song Sparrow is shy and retiring, content to make all the world glad with his song, but preferring to keep out of sight as much as possible.

Jenny chattered on as she hunted for some more material for her nest. "I suppose you've noticed," said she, "that he and his wife dress very much alike. They don't go in for bright colors any more than we Wrens do. They show good taste. I like the little brown caps they wear, and the way their breasts and sides are streaked with brown. Then, too, they are such useful folks. It is a pity that that nuisance of a Bully doesn't learn something from them. I suppose they stay rather later than we do in the fall."

"Yes," replied Peter. "They don't go until Jack Frost makes them. I don't know of any one that we miss more than we do them."

"Speaking of the sparrow family, did you see anything of Whitethroat?" asked Jenny Wren, as she rested for a moment in the doorway of her new house and looked down at Peter Rabbit.

Peter's face brightened. "I should say I did!" he exclaimed. "He stopped for a few days on his way north. I only wish he would stay here all the time. But he seems to think there is no place like the Great Woods of the North. I could listen all day to his song. Do you know what he always seems to be saying?"

"What?" demanded Jenny.

"I live happ-i-ly, happ-i-ly, happ-i-ly," replied Peter. "I guess he must too, because he makes other people so happy."

Jenny nodded in her usual emphatic way. "I don't know him as well as I do some of the others," said she, "but when I have seen him down in the South he always has appeared to me to be a perfect gentleman. He is social, too; he likes to travel with others."

"I've noticed that," said Peter. "He almost always has company when he passes through here. Some of those Sparrows are so much alike that it is hard for me to tell them apart, but I can always tell Whitethroat because he is one of the largest of the tribe and has such a lovely white throat. He really is handsome with his black and white cap and that bright yellow spot before each eye. I am told that he is very dearly loved up in the north where he makes his home. They say he sings all the time."

"I suppose Scratcher the Fox Sparrow has been along too," said Jenny. "He also started sometime before we did."

"Yes," replied Peter. "He spent one night in the dear Old Briar-patch. He is fine looking too, the biggest of all the Sparrow tribe, and *how* he can sing. The only thing I've got against him is the color of his coat. It always reminds me of Reddy Fox, and I don't like anything that reminds me of that fellow. When he visited us I discovered something about Scratcher which I don't believe you know."

"What?" demanded Jenny rather sharply.

"That when he scratches among the leaves he uses both feet at once," cried Peter triumphantly. "It's funny to watch him."

"Pooh! I knew that," retorted Jenny Wren. "What do you suppose my eyes are make for? I thought you were going to tell me something I didn't know."

Peter looked disappointed.

IV. Chippy, Sweetvoice, and Dotty.

For a while Jenny Wren was too busy to talk save to scold Mr. Wren for spending so much time singing instead of working. To Peter it seemed as if they were trying to fill that tree trunk with rubbish. "I should think they had enough stuff in there for half a dozen nests," muttered Peter. "I do believe they are carrying it in for the fun of working." Peter wasn't far wrong in this thought, as he was to discover a little later in the season when he found Mr. Wren building another nest for which he had no use.

Finding that for the time being he could get nothing more from Jenny Wren, Peter hopped over to visit Johnny Chuck, whose home was between the roots of an old apple-tree in the far corner of the Old Orchard. Peter was still thinking of the Sparrow family; what a big family it was, yet how seldom any of them, excepting Bully the English Sparrow, were to be found in the Old Orchard.

"Hello, Johnny Chuck!" cried Peter, as he discovered Johnny sitting on his doorstep. "You've lived in the Old Orchard a long time, so you ought to be able to tell me something I want to know. Why is it that none of the Sparrow family excepting that noisy nuisance, Bully, build in the trees of the Old Orchard? Is it because Bully has driven all the rest out?"

Johnny Chuck shook his head. "Peter," said he, "whatever is the matter with your ears? And whatever is the matter with your eyes?"

"Nothing," replied Peter rather shortly. "They are as good as yours any day, Johnny Chuck."

Johnny grinned. "Listen!" said Johnny. Peter listened. From

DOTTY THE TREE SPARROW. The reddish-brown cap and dark spot in the middle of his breast are all you need to look for.
SLATY THE JUNCO. The little slate-colored and white ground bird of winter.

a tree just a little way off came a clear "Chip, chip, chip, chip." Peter didn't need to be told to look. He knew without looking who was over there. He knew that voice for that of one of his oldest and best friends in the Old Orchard, a little fellow with a red-brown cap, brown back with feathers streaked with black, brownish wings and tail, a gray waistcoat and black bill, and a little white line over each eye—altogether as trim a little gentleman as Peter was acquainted with. It was Chippy, as everybody calls the Chipping Sparrow, the smallest of the family.

Peter looked a little foolish. "I forgot all about Chippy," said he. "Now I think of it, I have found Chippy here in the Old Orchard ever since I can remember. I never have seen his nest because I never happened to think about looking for it. Does he build a trashy nest like his cousin, Bully?"

Johnny Chuck laughed. "I should say not!" he exclaimed. "Twice Chippy and Mrs. Chippy have built their nest in this very old apple-tree. There is no trash in their nest, I can tell you! It is just as dainty as they are, and not a bit bigger than it has to be. It is made mostly of little fine, dry roots, and it is lined inside with horse-hair."

"What's that?" Peter's voice sounded as if he suspected that Johnny Chuck was trying to fool him.

"It's a fact," said Johnny, nodding his head gravely. "Goodness knows where they find it these days, but find it they do. Here comes Chippy himself; ask him."

Chippy and Mrs. Chippy came flitting from tree to tree until they were on a branch right over Peter and Johnny. "Hello!" cried Peter. "You folks seem very busy. Haven't you finished building your nest yet?"

"Nearly," replied Chippy. "It is all done but the horsehair. We are on our way up to Farmer Brown's barnyard now to look for some. You haven't seen any around anywhere, have you?"

Peter and Johnny shook their heads, and Peter confessed that he wouldn't know horsehair if he saw it. He often had found hair from the coats of Reddy Fox and Old Man Coyote and Digger the Badger and Lightfoot the Deer, but hair from the coat of a horse was altogether another matter.

"It isn't hair from the coat of a horse that we want," cried

Chippy, as he prepared to fly after Mrs. Chippy. “It is long hair from the tail or mane of a horse that we must have. It makes the very nicest kind of lining for a nest.”

Chippy and Mrs. Chippy were gone a long time, but when they did return each was carrying a long black hair. They had found what they wanted, and Mrs. Chippy was in high spirits because, as she took pains to explain to Peter, that little nest would not soon be ready for the four beautiful little blue eggs with black spots on one end she meant to lay in it.

“I just love Chippy and Mrs. Chippy,” said Peter, as they watched their two little feathered friends putting the finishing touches to the little nest far out on a branch of one of the apple-trees.

“Everybody does,” replied Johnny. “Everybody loves them as much as they hate Bully and his wife. Did you know that they are sometimes called Tree Sparrows? I suppose it is because they so often build their nests in trees?”

“No,” said Peter, “I didn’t. Chippy shouldn’t be called Tree Sparrow, because he has a cousin by that name.”

Johnny Chuck looked as if he doubted that, “I never heard of him,” he grunted.

Peter grinned. Here was a chance to tell Johnny Chuck something, and Peter never is happier than when he can tell folks something they don’t know. “You’d know him if you didn’t sleep all winter,” said Peter. “Dotty the Tree Sparrow spends the winter here. He left for his home in the Far North about the time you took it into your head to wake up.”

“Why do you call him Dotty?” asked Johnny Chuck.

“Because he has a little round black dot right in the middle of his breast,” replied Peter. “I don’t know why they call him Tree Sparrow; he doesn’t spend his time in the trees the way Chippy does, but I see him much oftener in low bushes or on the ground. I think Chippy has much more right to the name of Tree Sparrow than Dotty has. Now I think of it, I’ve heard Dotty called the Winter Chippy.”

“Gracious, what a mix-up!” exclaimed Johnny Chuck. “With Chippy being called a Tree Sparrow and a Tree Sparrow called Chippy, I should think folks would get all tangled up.”

"Perhaps they would," replied Peter, "if both were here at the same time, but Chippy comes just as Dotty goes, and Dotty comes as Chippy goes. That's a pretty good arrangement, especially as they look very much alike, excepting that Dotty is quite a little bigger than Chippy and always has that black dot, which Chippy does not have. Goodness gracious, it is time I was back in the dear Old Briar-patch! Good-by, Johnny Chuck."

Away went Peter Rabbit, lipperty-lipperty-lip, heading for the dear Old Briar-patch. Out of the grass just ahead of him flew a rather pale, streaked little brown bird, and as he spread his tail Peter saw two white feathers on the outer edges. Those two white feathers were all Peter needed to recognize another little friend of whom he is very fond. It was Sweetvoice the Vesper Sparrow, the only one of the Sparrow family with white feathers in his tail.

"Come over to the dear Old Briar-patch and sing to me," cried Peter.

Sweetvoice dropped down into the grass again, and when Peter came up, was very busy getting a mouthful of dry grass. "Can't," mumbled Sweetvoice. "Can't do it now, Peter Rabbit. I'm too busy. It is high time our nest was finished, and Mrs. Sweetvoice will lose her patience if I don't get this grass over there pretty quick."

"Where is your nest; in a tree?" asked Peter innocently.

"That's telling," declared Sweetvoice. "Not a living soul knows where that nest is, excepting Mrs. Sweetvoice and myself. This much I will tell you, Peter: it isn't in a tree. And I'll tell you this much more: it is in a hoofprint of Bossy the Cow."

"In a *what*?" cried Peter.

"In a hoofprint of Bossy the Cow," repeated Sweetvoice, chuckling softly. "You know when the ground was wet and soft early this spring, Bossy left deep footprints wherever she went. One of these makes the nicest kind of a place for a nest. I think we have picked out the very best one on all the Green Meadows. Now run along, Peter Rabbit, and don't bother me any more. I've got too much to do to sit here talking. Perhaps I'll come over to the edge of the dear Old Briar-patch and sing to you a while just after jolly, round, red Mr. Sun goes to bed

SWEET VOICE THE VESPER SPARROW. You can tell him from other Sparrows by the white outer feathers of his tail.

LITTLE FRIEND THE SONG SPARROW. His tinkling, happy song can never be mistaken.

behind the Purple Hills. I just love to sing then."

"I'll be watching for you," replied Peter. "You don't love to sing any better than I love to hear you. I think that is the best time of all the day in which to sing. I mean, I think it's the best time to hear singing," for of course Peter himself does not sing at all.

That night, sure enough, just as the Black Shadows came creeping out over the Green Meadows, Sweetvoice, perched on the top of a bramble-bush over Peter's head, sang over and over again the sweetest little song and kept on singing even after it was quite dark. Peter didn't know it, but it is this habit of singing in the evening which has given Sweetvoice his name of Vesper Sparrow.

V. Peter Learns Something He Hadn't Guessed.

Running over to the Old Orchard very early in the morning for a little gossip with Jenny Wren and his other friends there had become a regular thing with Peter Rabbit. He was learning a great many things, and some of them were most surprising.

Now two of Peter's oldest and best friends in the Old Orchard were Winsome Bluebird and Welcome Robin. Every spring they arrived pretty nearly together, though Winsome Bluebird usually was a few days ahead of Welcome Robin. This year Winsome had arrived while the snow still lingered in patches. He was, as he always is, the herald of sweet Mistress Spring. And when Peter had heard for the first time Winsome's soft, sweet whistle, which seemed to come from nowhere in particular and from everywhere in general, he had kicked up his long hind legs from pure joy. Then, when a few days later he had heard Welcome Robin's joyous message of "Cheer-up! Cheer-up! Cheer-up! Cheer-up! Cheer!" from the tiptop of a tall tree, he had known that Mistress Spring really had arrived.

Peter loves Winsome Bluebird and Welcome Robin, just as everybody else does, and he had known them so long and so well that he thought he knew all there was to know about them. He would have been very indignant had anybody told him he didn't.

"Those cousins don't look much alike, do they?" remarked Jenny Wren, as she poked her head out of her house to gossip with Peter.

"What cousins?" demanded Peter, staring very hard in the direction in which Jenny Wren was looking.

"Those two sitting on the fence over there. Where are your eyes, Peter?" replied Jenny rather sharply.

WELCOME ROBIN. No other bird has a russet breast like his.
WINSOME BLUEBIRD. His blue back, wings and tail leave no doubt as to who he is.

Peter stared harder than ever. On one post sat Winsome Bluebird, and on another post sat Welcome Robin. "I don't see anybody but Winsome and Welcome, and they are not even related," replied Peter with a little puzzled frown.

"Tut, tut, tut, tut, tut, Peter!" exclaimed Jenny Wren. "Tut, tut, tut, tut, tut! Who told you any such nonsense as that? Of course they are related. They are cousins. I thought everybody knew that. They belong to the same family that Melody the Thrush and all the other Thrushes belong to. That makes them all cousins."

"What?" exclaimed Peter, looking as if he didn't believe a word of what Jenny Wren had said. Jenny repeated, and still Peter looked doubtful.

Then Jenny lost her temper, a thing she does very easily. "If you don't believe me, go ask one of them," she snapped, and disappeared inside her house, where Peter could hear her scolding away to herself.

The more he thought of it, the more this struck Peter as good advice. So he hopped over to the foot of the fence post on which Winsome Bluebird was sitting. "Jenny Wren says that you and Welcome Robin are cousins. She doesn't know what she is talking about, does she?" asked Peter.

Winsome chuckled. It was a soft, gentle chuckle. "Yes," said he, nodding his head, "we are. You can trust that little busybody to know what she is talking about, every time. I sometimes think she knows more about other people's affairs than about her own. Welcome and I may not look much alike, but we are cousins just the same. Don't you think Welcome is looking unusually fine this spring?"

"Not a bit finer than you are yourself, Winsome," replied Peter politely. "I just love that sky-blue coat of yours. What is the reason that Mrs. Bluebird doesn't wear as bright a coat as you do?"

"Go ask Jenny Wren," chuckled Winsome Bluebird, and before Peter could say another word he flew over to the roof of Farmer Brown's house.

Back scampered Peter to tell Jenny Wren that he was sorry he had doubted her and that he never would again. Then he begged Jenny to tell him why it was that Mrs. Bluebird was not as brightly dressed as was Winsome.

"Mrs. Bluebird, like most mothers, is altogether too busy to spend much time taking care of her clothes; and fine clothes need a lot of care," replied Jenny. "Besides, when Winsome is about he attracts all the attention and that gives her a chance to slip in and out of her nest without being noticed. I don't believe you know, Peter Rabbit, where Winsome's nest is."

Peter had to admit that he didn't, although he had tried his best to find out by watching Winsome. "I think it's over in that little house put up by Farmer Brown's boy," he ventured. "I saw both Mr. and Mrs. Bluebird go in it when they first came, and I've seen Winsome around it a great deal since, so I guess it is there."

"So you guess it is there!" mimicked Jenny Wren. "Well, your guess is quite wrong, Peter; quite wrong. As a matter of fact, it is in one of those old fence posts. But just which one I am not going to tell you. I will leave that for you to find out. Mrs. Bluebird certainly shows good sense. She knows a good house when she sees it. The hole in that post is one of the best holes anywhere around here. If I had arrived here early enough I would have taken it myself. But Mrs. Bluebird already had her nest built in it and four eggs there, so there was nothing for me to do but come here. Just between you and me, Peter, I think the Bluebirds show more sense in nest building than do their cousins the Robins. There is nothing like a house with stout walls and a doorway just big enough to get in and out of comfortably."

Peter nodded quite as if he understood all about the advantages of a house with walls. "That reminds me," said he. "The other day I saw Welcome Robin getting mud and carrying it away. Pretty soon he was joined by Mrs. Robin, and she did the same thing. They kept it up till I got tired of watching them. What were they doing with that mud?"

"Building their nest, of course, stupid," retorted Jenny. "Welcome Robin, with that black head, beautiful russet breast, black and white throat and yellow bill, not to mention the proud way in which he carries himself, certainly is a handsome fellow, and Mrs. Robin is only a little less handsome. How they can be content to build the kind of a home they do is more than I can understand. People think that Mr. Wren and I use a lot of trash in our nest. Perhaps we do, but I can tell you one thing, and that is it is clean trash. It is just sticks and clean straws, and before I lay my eggs I see to it that my nest is lined with feathers. More than this, there isn't any cleaner housekeeper than I am, if I do say it.

"Welcome Robin is a fine looker and a fine singer, and everybody loves him. But when it comes to housekeeping, he and Mrs. Robin are just plain dirty. They make the foundation of their nest of mud,—plain, common, ordinary mud. They cover this with dead grass, and sometimes there is mighty little of this over the inside walls of mud. I know because I've seen the inside of their nest often. Anybody with any eyes at all can find their nest. More than once I've known them to have their nest washed away in a heavy rain, or have it blown down in a high wind. Nothing like that ever happens to Winsome Bluebird or to me."

Jenny disappeared inside her house, and Peter waited for her to come out again. Welcome Robin flew down on the ground, ran a few steps, and then stood still with his head on one side as if listening. Then he reached down and tugged at something, and presently out of the ground came a long, wriggling angleworm. Welcome gulped it down and ran on a few steps, then once more paused to listen. This time he turned and ran three or four steps to the right, where he pulled another worm out of the ground.

"He acts as if he heard those worms in the ground," said Peter, speaking aloud without thinking.

"He does," said Jenny Wren, poking her head out of her doorway just as Peter spoke. "How do you suppose he would find them when they are in the ground if he didn't hear them?"

"Can you hear them?" asked Peter.

"I've never tried, and I don't intend to waste my time trying," retorted Jenny. "Welcome Robin may enjoy eating them, but for my part I want something smaller and daintier, young grasshoppers, tender young beetles, small caterpillars, bugs and spiders."

Peter had to turn his head aside to hide the wry face he just had to make at the mention of such things as food. "Is that all Welcome Robin eats?" he asked innocently.

"I should say not," laughed Jenny. "He eats a lot of other kinds of worms, and he just dearly loves fruit like strawberries and cherries and all sorts of small berries. Well, I can't stop here talking any longer. I'm going to tell you a secret, Peter, if you'll promise not to tell."

Of course Peter promised, and Jenny leaned so far down that Peter wondered how she could keep from falling as she whispered, "I've got seven eggs in my nest, so if you don't see much of me for the next week or more, you'll know why. I've just got to sit on those eggs and keep them warm."

VI. AN OLD FRIEND IN A NEW HOME.

EVERY DAY brought newcomers to the Old Orchard, and early in the morning there were so many voices to be heard that perhaps it is no wonder if for some time Peter Rabbit failed to miss that of one of his very good friends. Most unexpectedly he was reminded of this as very early one morning he scampered, lipperty-lipperty-lip, across a little bridge over the Laughing Brook.

"Dear me! Dear me! Dear me!" cried rather a plaintive voice. Peter stopped so suddenly that he all but fell heels over head. Sitting on the top of a tall, dead, mullein stalk was a very soberly dressed but rather trim little fellow, a very little larger than Bully the English Sparrow. Above, his coat was of a dull olive-brown, while underneath he was of a grayish-white, with faint tinges of yellow in places. His head was dark, and his bill black. The feathers on his head were lifted just enough to make the tiniest kind of crest. His wings and tail were dusky, little bars of white showing very faintly on his wings, while the outer edges of his tail were distinctly white. He sat with his tail hanging straight down, as if he hadn't strength enough to hold it up.

"Hello, Dear Me!" cried Peter joyously. "What are you doing way down here? I haven't seen you since you first arrived, just after Winsome Bluebird got here." Peter started to say that he had wondered what had become of Dear Me, but checked himself, for Peter is very honest and he realized now that in the excitement of greeting so many friends he hadn't missed Dear Me at all.

Dear Me the Phoebe did not reply at once, but darted out into the air, and Peter heard a sharp click of that little black bill.

Making a short circle, Dear Me alighted on the mullein stalk again.

"Did you catch a fly then?" asked Peter.

"Dear me! Dear me! Of course I did," was the prompt reply. And with each word there was a jerk of that long hanging tail. Peter almost wondered if in some way Dear Me's tongue and tail were connected. "I suppose," said he, "that it is the habit of catching flies and bugs in the air that has given your family the name of Flycatchers."

Dear Me nodded and almost at once started into the air again. Once more Peter heard the click of that little black bill, then Dear Me was back on his perch. Peter asked again what he was doing down there.

"Mrs. Phoebe and I are living down here," replied Dear Me. "We've made our home down here and we like it very much."

Peter looked all around, this way, that way, every way, with the funniest expression on his face. He didn't see anything of Mrs. Phoebe and he didn't see any place in which he could imagine Mr. and Mrs. Phoebe building a nest. "What are you looking for?" asked Dear Me.

"For Mrs. Phoebe and your home," declared Peter quite frankly. "I didn't suppose you and Mrs. Phoebe ever built a nest on the ground, and I don't see any other place around here for one."

Dear Me chuckled. "I wouldn't tell any one but you, Peter," said he, "but I've known you so long that I'm going to let you into a little secret. Mrs. Phoebe and our home are under the very bridge you are sitting on."

"I don't believe it!" cried Peter.

But Dear Me knew from the way Peter said it that he really didn't mean that. "Look and see for yourself," said Dear Me.

So Peter lay flat on his stomach and tried to stretch his head over the edge of the bridge so as to see under it. But his neck wasn't long enough, or else he was afraid to lean over as far as he might have. Finally he gave up and at Mr. Phoebe's suggestion crept down the bank to the very edge of the Laughing Brook. Dear Me darted out to catch another fly, then flew right in under the bridge and alighted on a little ledge of stone just beneath the floor. There, sure enough, was a nest, and Peter could see Mrs. Phoebe's bill and the top of her head above the edge of it.

CHEBEC THE LEAST FLYCATCHER. He will tell you his name.
DEAR ME THE PHOEBE. Look for him around an old bridge or shed.

It was a nest with a foundation of mud covered with moss and lined with feathers.

"That's perfectly splendid!" cried Peter, as Dear Me resumed his perch on the old mullein stalk. "How did you ever come to think of such a place? And why did you leave the shed up at Farmer Brown's where you have build your home for the last two or three years?"

"Oh," replied Dear Me, "we Phoebes always have been fond of building under bridges. You see a place like this is quite safe. Then, too, we like to be near water. Always there are many insects flying around where there is water, so it is an easy matter to get plenty to eat. I left the shed at Farmer Brown's because that pesky cat up there discovered our nest last year, and we had a dreadful time keeping our babies out of her clutches. She hasn't found us down here, and she wouldn't be able to trouble us if she should find us."

"I suppose," said Peter, "that as usual you were the first of your family to arrive."

"Certainly. Of course," replied Dear Me. "We always are the first. Mrs. Phoebe and I don't go as far south in winter as the other members of the family do. They go clear down into the Tropics, but we manage to pick up a pretty good living without going as far as that. So we get back here before the rest of them, and usually have begun housekeeping by the time they arrive. My cousin, Chebec the Least Flycatcher, should be here by this time. Haven't you heard anything of him up in the Old Orchard?"

"No," replied Peter, "but to tell the truth I haven't looked for him. I'm on my way to the Old Orchard now, and I certainly shall keep my ears and eyes open for Chebec. I'll tell you if I find him. Good-by."

"Dear me! Dear me! Good-by Peter. Dear me!" replied Mr. Phoebe as Peter started off for the Old Orchard.

Perhaps it was because Peter was thinking of him that almost the first voice he heard when he reached the Old Orchard was that of Chebec, repeating his own name over and over as if he loved the sound of it. It didn't take Peter long to find him. He was sitting out on the up of one of the upper branches of an apple-tree where he could watch for flies and other winged insects.

He looked so much like Mr. Phoebe, save that he was smaller, that any one would have know they were cousins. "Chebec! Chebec! Chebec!" he repeated over and over, and with every note jerked his tail. Now and then he would dart out into the air and snap up something so small that Peter, looking up from the ground, couldn't see it at all.

"Hello, Chebec!" cried Peter. "I'm glad to see you back again. Are you going to build in the Old Orchard this year?"

"Of course I am," replied Chebec promptly. "Mrs. Chebec and I have built here for the last two or three years, and we wouldn't think of going anywhere else. Mrs. Chebec is looking for a place now. I suppose I ought to be helping her, but I learned a long time ago, Peter Rabbit, that in matters of this kind it is just as well not to have any opinion at all. When Mrs. Chebec has picked out just the place she wants, I'll help her build the nest. It certainly is good to be back here in the Old Orchard and planning a home once more. We've made a terribly long journey, and I for one am glad it's over."

"I just saw your cousins, Mr. and Mrs. Phoebe, and they already have a nest and eggs," said Peter.

"The Phoebes are a funny lot," replied Chebec. "They are the only members of the family that can stand cold weather. What pleasure they get out of it I don't understand. They are queer anyway, for they never build their nests in trees as the rest of us do."

"Are you the smallest in the family?" asked Peter, for it had suddenly struck him that Chebec was a very little fellow indeed.

Chebec nodded. "I'm the smallest," said he. "That's why they call me Least Flycatcher. I may be least in size, but I can tell you one thing, Peter Rabbit, and that is that I can catch just as many bugs and flies as any of them." Suiting action to the word, he darted out into the air. His little bill snapped and with a quick turn he was back on his former perch, jerking his tail and uttering his sharp little cry of, "Chebec! Chebec! Chebec!" until Peter began to wonder which he was the most fond of, catching flies, or the sound of his own voice.

Presently they both heard Mrs. Chebec calling from somewhere in the middle of the Old Orchard. "Excuse me, Peter," said Chebec, "I must go at once. Mrs. Chebec says she has found just the place for our nest, and now we've got a busy time ahead of us. We are very particular how we build a nest."

"Do you start it with mud the way Welcome Robin and your cousins, the Phoebes, do?" asked Peter.

"Mud!" cried Chebec scornfully. "Mud! I should say not! I would have you understand, Peter, that we are very particular about what we use in our nest. We use only the finest of rootlets, strips of soft bark, fibers of plants, the brown cotton that grows on ferns, and perhaps a little hair when we can find it. We make a dainty nest, if I do say it, and we fasten it securely in the fork made by two or three upright little branches. Now I must go because Mrs. Chebec is getting impatient. Come see me when I'm not so busy Peter."

VII. THE WATCHMAN OF THE OLD ORCHARD.

A FEW days after Chebec and his wife started building their nest in the Old Orchard Peter dropped around as usual for a very early call. He found Chebec very busy hunting for materials for that nest, because, as he explained to Peter, Mrs. Chebec is very particular indeed about what her nest is made of. But he had time to tell Peter a bit of news.

"My fighting cousin and my handsomest cousin arrived together yesterday, and now our family is very well represented in the Old Orchard," said Chebec proudly.

Slowly Peter reached over his back with his long left hind foot and thoughtfully scratched his long right ear. He didn't like to admit that he couldn't recall those two cousins of Chebec's. "Did you say your fighting cousin?" he asked in a hesitating way.

"That's what I said," replied Chebec. "He is Scrapper the Kingbird, as of course you know. The rest of us always feel safe when he is about."

"Of course I know him," declared Peter, his face clearing. "Where is he now?"

At that very instant a great racket broke out on the other side of the Old Orchard and in no time at all the feathered folks were hurrying from every direction, screaming at the top of their voices. Of course, Peter couldn't be left out of anything like that, and he scampered for the scene of trouble as fast as his legs could take him. When he got there he saw Redtail the Hawk flying up and down and this way and that way, as if trying to get away from something or somebody.

For a minute Peter couldn't think what was the trouble with Redtail, and then he saw. A white-throated, white-breasted bird,

SCRAPPER THE KINGBIRD. Look in the Old Orchard for a bird with white breast, dark head and back, and with a white tip to his tail.
REDEYE THE VIREO. The only Vireo with red eyes.

having a black cap and back, and a broad white band across the end of his tail, was darting at Redtail as if he meant to pull out every feather in the latter's coat.

He was just a little smaller than Welcome Robin, and in comparison with him Redtail was a perfect giant. But this seemed to make no difference to Scrapper, for that is who it was. He wasn't afraid, and he intended that everybody should know it, especially Redtail. It is because of his fearlessness that he is called Kingbird. All the time he was screaming at the top of his lungs, calling Redtail a robber and every other bad name he could think of. All the other birds joined him in calling Redtail bad names. But none, not even Bully the English Sparrow, was brave enough to join him in attacking big Redtail.

When he had succeeded in driving Redtail far enough from the Old Orchard to suit him, Scrapper flew back and perched on a dead branch of one of the trees, where he received the congratulations of all his feathered neighbors. He took them quite modestly, assuring them that he had done nothing, nothing at all, but that he didn't intend to have any of the Hawk family around the Old Orchard while he lived there. Peter couldn't help but admire Scrapper for his courage.

As Peter looked up at Scrapper he saw that, like all the rest of the flycatchers, there was just the tiniest of hooks on the end of his bill. Scrapper's slightly raised cap seemed all black, but if Peter could have gotten close enough, he would have found that hidden in it was a patch of orange-red. While Peter sat staring up at him Scrapper suddenly darted out into the air, and his bill snapped in quite the same way Chebec's did when he caught a fly. But it wasn't a fly that Scrapper had. It was a bee. Peter saw it very distinctly just as Scrapper snapped it up. It reminded Peter that he had often heard Scrapper called the Bee Martin, and now he understood why.

"Do you live on bees altogether?" asked Peter.

"Bless your heart, Peter, no," replied Scrapper with a chuckle. "There wouldn't be any honey if I did. I like bees. I like them first rate. But they form only a very small part of my food. Those that I do catch are mostly drones, and you know the drones are useless. They do no work at all. It is only by accident that I now and then catch a worker. I eat all kinds of insects that fly and some that don't. I'm one of Farmer Brown's best friends, if he did but know it. You can talk all you please about the wonderful eyesight of the members of the Hawk family, but if any one of them has better eyesight than I have, I'd like to know who it is. There's a fly 'way over there beyond that old apple-tree; watch me catch it."

Peter knew better than to waste any effort trying to see that fly. He knew that he couldn't have seen it had it been only one fourth that distance away. But if he couldn't see the fly he could hear the sharp click of Scrapper's bill, and he knew by the way Scrapper kept opening and shutting his mouth after his return that he had caught that fly and it had tasted good.

"Are you going to build in the Old Orchard this year?" asked Peter.

"Of course I am," declared Scrapper. "I—"

Just then he spied Blacky the Crow and dashed out to meet him. Blacky saw him coming and was wise enough to suddenly appear to have no interest whatever in the Old Orchard, turning away toward the Green Meadows instead.

Peter didn't wait for Scrapper to return. It was getting high time for him to scamper home to the dear Old Briar-patch and so he started along, lipperty-lipperty-lip. Just as he was leaving the far corner of the Old Orchard some one called him. "Peter! Oh, Peter Rabbit!" called the voice. Peter stopped abruptly, sat up very straight, looked this way, looked that way and looked the other way, every way but the right way.

"Look up over your head," cried the voice, rather a harsh voice. Peter looked, then all in a flash it came to him who it was Chebec had meant by the handsomest member of his family. It was Cresty the Great Crested Flycatcher. He was a wee bit bigger than Scrapper the Kingbird, yet not quite so big as Welcome Robin, and more slender. His throat and breast were gray, shading into bright yellow underneath. His back and head were of a grayish-brown with a tint of olive-green. A pointed cap was all that was needed to make him quite distinguished looking. He certainly was the handsomest as well as the largest of the Flycatcher family.

"You seem to be in a hurry, so don't let me detain you, Peter," said Cresty, before Peter could find his tongue. "I just want to ask one little favor of you."

"What is it?" asked Peter, who is always glad to do any one a favor.

"If in your roaming about you run across an old cast-off suit of Mr. Black Snake, or of any other member of the Snake family, I wish you would remember me and let me know. Will you, Peter?" said Cresty.

"A—a—a—what?" stammered Peter.

"A cast-off suit of clothes from any member of the Snake family," replied Cresty somewhat impatiently. "Now don't forget, Peter. I've got to go house hunting, but you'll find me there or hereabouts, if it happens that you find one of those cast-off Snake suits."

Before Peter could say another word Cresty had flown away. Peter hesitated, looking first towards the dear Old Briar-patch and then towards Jenny Wren's house. He just couldn't understand about those cast-off suits of the Snake family, and he felt sure that Jenny Wren could tell him. Finally curiosity got the best of him, and back he scampered, lipperty-lipperty-lip, to the foot of the tree in which Jenny Wren had her home.

"Jenny!" called Peter. "Jenny Wren! Jenny Wren!" No one answered him. He could hear Mr. Wren singing in another tree, but he couldn't see him. "Jenny! Jenny Wren! Jenny Wren!" called Peter again. This time Jenny popped her head out, and her little eyes fairly snapped. "Didn't I tell you the other day, Peter Rabbit, that I'm not to be disturbed? Didn't I tell you that I've got seven eggs in here, and that I can't spend any time gossiping? Didn't I, Peter Rabbit? Didn't I? Didn't I?"

"You certainly did, Jenny. You certainly did, and I'm sorry to disturb you," replied Peter meekly. "I wouldn't have thought of doing such a thing, but I just didn't know who else to go to."

"Go to for what?" snapped Jenny Wren. "What is it you've come to me for?"

"Snake skins," replied Peter.

"Snake skins! Snake skins!" shrieked Jenny Wren. "What are you talking about, Peter Rabbit? I never have anything to do with Snake skins and don't want to. Ugh! It makes me shiver just to think of it."

"You don't understand," cried Peter hurriedly. "What I want to know is, why should Cresty the Flycatcher ask me to please let him know if I found any cast-off suits of the Snake family? He flew away before I could ask him why he wants them, and so I came to you, because I know you know everything, especially everything concerning your neighbors."

Jenny Wren looked as if she didn't know whether to feel flattered or provoked. But Peter looked so innocent that she concluded he was trying to say something nice.

VIII. Old Clothes and Old Houses.

"I can't stop to talk to you any longer now, Peter Rabbit," said Jenny Wren, "but if you will come over here bright and early to-morrow morning, while I am out to get my breakfast, I will tell you about Cresty the Flycatcher and why he wants the cast-off clothes of some of the Snake family. Perhaps I should say *what* he wants of them instead of *why* he wants them, for why any one should want anything to do with Snakes is more then I can understand."

With this Jenny Wren disappeared inside her house, and there was nothing for Peter to do but once more start for the dear Old Briar-patch. On his way he couldn't resist the temptation to run over to the Green Forest, which was just beyond the Old Orchard. He just *had* to find out if there was anything new over there. Hardly had he reached it when he heard a plaintive voice crying, "Pee-wee! Pee-wee! Pee-wee!" Peter chuckled happily. "I declare, there's Pee-wee," he cried. "He usually is one of the last of the Flycatcher family to arrive. I didn't expect to find him yet. I wonder what has brought him up so early."

It didn't take Peter long to find Pewee. He just followed the sound of that voice and presently saw Pewee fly out and make the same kind of a little circle as the other members of the family make when they are hunting flies. It ended just where it had started, on a dead twig of a tree in a shady, rather lonely part of the Green Forest. Almost at once he began to call his name in a rather sad, plaintive tone, "Pee-wee! Pee-wee! Pee-wee!" But he wasn't sad, as Peter well knew. It was his way of expressing how happy he felt. He was a little bigger than his cousin, Chebec, but looked very much like him. There was a little notch in the end of his tail. The upper half of his bill was black, but the lower half was light. Peter could see on each wing two whitish bars, and he noticed that Pewee's wings were longer than his tail, which wasn't the case with Chebec. But no one could ever mistake Pewee for any of his relatives, for the simple reason that he keeps repeating his own name over and over.

"Aren't you here early?" asked Peter.

Pewee nodded. "Yes," said he. "It has been unusually warm this spring, so I hurried a little and came up with my cousins, Scrapper and Cresty. That is something I don't often do."

"If you please," Peter inquired politely, "why do folks call you Wood Pewee?"

Pewee chuckled happily. "It must be," said he, "because I am so very fond of the Green Forest. It is so quiet and restful that I love it. Mrs. Pewee and I are very retiring. We do not like too many near neighbors."

"You won't mind if I come to see you once in a while, will you?" asked Peter as he prepared to start on again for the dear Old Briar-patch.

"Come as often as you like," replied Pewee. "The oftener the better."

Back in the Old Briar-patch Peter thought over all he had learned about the Flycatcher family, and as he recalled how they were forever catching all sorts of flying insects it suddenly struck him that they must be very useful little people in helping Old Mother Nature take care of her trees and other growing things which insects so dearly love to destroy.

But most of all Peter thought about that queer request of Cresty's, and a dozen times that day he found himself peeping under old logs in the hope of finding a cast-off coat of Mr. Black Snake. It was such a funny thing for Cresty to ask for that Peter's curiosity would allow him no peace, and the next morning he was up in the Old Orchard before jolly Mr. Sun had kicked his bedclothes off.

Jenny Wren was as good as her word. While she flitted and hopped about this way and that way in that fussy way of hers, getting her breakfast, she talked. Jenny couldn't keep her tongue still if she wanted to.

"Did you find any old clothes of the Snake family?" she demanded. Then as Peter shook his head her tongue ran on without waiting for him to reply. "Cresty and his wife always insist upon having a piece of Snake skin in their nest," said she. "Why they want it, goodness knows! But they do want it and never can seem to settle down to housekeeping unless they have it. Perhaps they think it will scare robbers away. As for me, I should have a cold chill every time I got into my nest if I had to sit on anything like that. I have to admit that Cresty and his wife are a handsome couple, and they certainly have good sense in choosing a house, more sense than any other member of their family to my way of thinking. But Snake skins! Ugh!"

"By the way, where does Cresty build?" asked Peter.

"In a hole in a tree, like the rest of us sensible people," retorted Jenny Wren promptly.

Peter looked quite as surprised as he felt. "Does Cresty make the hole?" he asked.

"Goodness gracious, no!" exclaimed Jenny Wren. "Where are your eyes, Peter? Did you ever see a Flycatcher with a bill that looked as if it could cut wood?" She didn't wait for a reply, but rattled on. "It is a good thing for a lot of us that the Woodpecker family are so fond of new houses. Look! There is Downy the Woodpecker hard at work on a new house this very minute. That's good. I like to see that. It means that next year there will be one more house for some one here in the Old Orchard. For myself I prefer old houses. I've noticed there are a number of my neighbors who feel the same way about it. There is something settled about an old house. It doesn't attract attention the way a new one does. So long as it has got reasonably good walls, and the rain and the wind can't get in, the older it is the better it suits me. But the Woodpeckers seem to like new houses best, which, as I said before, is a very good thing for the rest of us."

"Who is there besides you and Cresty and Bully the English Sparrow who uses these old Woodpecker houses?" asked Peter.

"Winsome Bluebird, stupid!" snapped Jenny Wren.

Peter grinned and looked foolish. "Of course," said he. "I forgot all about Winsome."

"And Skimmer the Tree Swallow," added Jenny.

"That's so; I ought to have remembered him," exclaimed Peter. "I've noticed that he is very fond of the same house year after year. Is there anybody else?"

Again Jenny Wren nodded. "Yank-Yank the Nuthatch uses an old house, I'm told, but he usually goes up North for his nesting," said she. "Tommy Tit the Chickadee sometimes uses an old house. Then again he and Mrs. Chickadee get fussy and make a house for themselves. Yellow Wing the flicker, who really is a Woodpecker, often uses an old house, but quite often makes a new one. Then there are Killy the Sparrow Hawk and Spooky the Screech Owl."

Peter looked surprised. "I didn't suppose *they* nested in holes in trees!" he exclaimed.

"They certainly do, more's the pity!" snapped Jenny. "It would be a good thing for the rest of us if they didn't nest at all. But they do, and an old house of Yellow Wing the Flicker suits either of them. Killy always uses one that is high up, and comes back to it year after year. Spooky isn't particular so long as the house is big enough to be comfortable. He lives in it more or less the year around. Now I must get back to those eggs of mine. I've talked quite enough for one morning."

"Oh, Jenny," cried Peter, as a sudden thought struck him.

Jenny paused and jerked her tail impatiently. "Well, what is it now?" she demanded.

"Have you got two homes?" asked Peter.

"Goodness gracious, no!" exclaimed Jenny. "What do you suppose I want of two homes? One is all I can take care of."

"Then why," demanded Peter triumphantly, "does Mr. Wren work all day carrying sticks and straws into a hole in another tree? It seems to me that he has carried enough in there to build two or three nests."

Jenny Wren's eyes twinkled, and she laughed softly. "Mr. Wren just has to be busy about something, bless his heart," said she. "He hasn't a lazy feather on him. He's building that nest to take up his time and keep out of mischief. Besides, if he fills that hollow up nobody else will take it, and you know we might want to move some time. Good-by, Peter." With a final jerk of her tail Jenny Wren flew to the little round doorway of her house and popped inside.

IX. LONGBILL AND TEETER.

FROM THE decided way in which Jenny Wren had popped into the little round doorway of her home, Peter knew that to wait in the hope of more gossip with her would be a waste of time. He wasn't ready to go back home to the dear Old Briar-patch, yet there seemed nothing else to do, for everybody in the Old Orchard was too busy for idle gossip. Peter scratched a long ear with a long hind foot, trying to think of some place to go. Just then he heard the clear "peep, peep, peep" of the Hylas, the sweet singers of the Smiling Pool.

"That's where I'll go!" exclaimed Peter. "I haven't been to the Smiling Pool for some time. I'll just run over and pay my respects to Grandfather Frog, and to Redwing the Blackbird. Redwing was one of the first birds to arrive, and I've neglected him shamefully."

When Peter thinks of something to do he wastes no time. Off he started, lipperty-lipperty-lip, for the Smiling Pool. He kept close to the edge of the Green Forest until he reached the place where the Laughing Brook comes out of the Green Forest on its way to the Smiling Pool in the Green Meadows. Bushes and young trees grow along the banks of the Laughing Brook at this point. The ground was soft in places, quite muddy. Peter doesn't mind getting his feet damp, so he hopped along carelessly. From right under his very nose something shot up into the air with a whistling sound. It startled Peter so that he stopped short with his eyes popping out of his head. He had just a glimpse of a brown form disappearing over the tops of some tall bushes. Then Peter chuckled. "I declare," said he, "I had forgotten all about my old friend, Longbill the Woodcock.

He scared me for a second."

"Then you are even," said a voice close at hand. "You scared him. I saw you coming, but Longbill didn't."

Peter turned quickly. There was Mrs. Woodcock peeping at him from behind a tussock of grass.

"I didn't mean to scare him," apologized Peter. "I really didn't mean to. Do you think he was really very much scared?"

"Not too scared to come back, anyway," said Longbill himself, dropping down just in front of Peter. "I recognized you just as I was disappearing over the tops of the bushes, so I came right back. I learned when I was very young that when startled it is best to fly first and find out afterwards whether or not there is real danger. I am glad it is no one but you, Peter, for I was having a splendid meal here, and I should have hated to leave it. You'll excuse me while I go on eating, I hope. We can talk between bites."

"Certainly I'll excuse you," replied Peter, staring around very hard to see what it could be Longbill was making such a good meal of. But Peter couldn't see a thing that looked good to eat. There wasn't even a bug or a worm crawling on the ground. Longbill took two or three steps in rather a stately fashion. Peter had to hide a smile, for Longbill had such an air of importance, yet at the same time was such an odd looking fellow. He was quite a little bigger than Welcome Robin, his tail was short, his legs were short, and his neck was short. But his bill was long enough to make up. His back was a mixture of gray, brown, black and buff, while his breast and under parts were a beautiful reddish-buff. It was his head that made him look queer. His eyes were very big and they were set so far back that Peter wondered if it wasn't easier for him to look behind him than in front of him.

Suddenly Longbill plunged his bill into the ground. He plunged it in for the whole length. Then he pulled it out and Peter caught a glimpse of the tail end of a worm disappearing down Longbill's throat. Where that long bill had gone into the ground was a neat little round hole. For the first time Peter noticed that there were many such little round holes all about. "Did you make all those little round holes?" exclaimed Peter.

"Not at all," replied Longbill. "Mrs. Woodcock made some

LONGBILL THE WOODCOCK. Look for him in damp, wooded places.

BOB WHITE. No other bird is shaped like him.

of them."

"And was there a worm in every one?" asked Peter, his eyes very wide with interest.

Longbill nodded. "Of course," said he. "You don't suppose we would take the trouble to bore one of them if we didn't know that we would get a worm at the end of it, do you?"

Peter remembered how he had watched Welcome Robin listen and then suddenly plunge his bill into the ground and pull out a worm. But the worms Welcome Robin got were always close to the surface, while these worms were so deep in the earth that Peter couldn't understand how it was possible for any one to know that they were there. Welcome Robin could see when he got hold of a worm, but Longbill couldn't. "Even if you know there is a worm down there in the ground, how do you know when you've reached him? And how is it possible for you to open your bill down there to take him in?" asked Peter.

Longbill chuckled. "That's easy," said he. "I've got the handiest bill that ever was. See here!" Longbill suddenly thrust his bill straight out in front of him and to Peter's astonishment he lifted the end of the upper half without opening the rest of his bill at all. "That's the way I get them," said he. "I can feel them when I reach them, and then I just open the top of my bill and grab them. I think there is one right under my feet now; watch me get him." Longbill bored into the ground until his head was almost against it. When he pulled his bill out, sure enough, there was a worm. "Of course," explained Longbill, "it is only in soft ground that I can do this. That is why I have to fly away south as soon as the ground freezes at all."

"It's wonderful," sighed Peter. "I don't suppose any one else can find hidden worms that way."

"My cousin, Jack Snipe, can," replied Longbill promptly. "He feeds the same way I do, only he likes marshy meadows instead of brushy swamps. Perhaps you know him."

Peter nodded. "I do," said he. "Now you speak of it, there is a strong family resemblance, although I hadn't thought of him as a relative of yours before. Now I must be running along. I'm ever so glad to have seen you, and I'm coming over to call again the first chance I get."

So Peter said good-by and kept on down the Laughing Brook to the Smiling Pool. Right where the Laughing Brook entered the Smiling Pool there was a little pebbly beach. Running along the very edge of the water was a slim, trim little bird with fairly long legs, a long slender bill, brownish-gray back with black spots and markings, and a white waistcoat neatly spotted with black. Every few steps he would stop to pick up something, then stand for a second bobbing up and down in the funniest way, as if his body was so nicely balanced on his legs that it teetered back and forth like a seesaw. It was Teeter the Spotted Sandpiper, an old friend of Peter's. Peter greeted him joyously.

"Peet-weet! Peet-weet!" cried Teeter, turning towards Peter and bobbing and bowing as only Teeter can. Before Peter could say another word Teeter came running towards him, and it was plain to see that Teeter was very anxious about something. "Don't move, Peter Rabbit! Don't move!" he cried.

"Why not?" demanded Peter, for he could see no danger and could think of no reason why he shouldn't move. Just then Mrs. Teeter came hurrying up and squatted down in the sand right in front of Peter.

"Thank goodness!" exclaimed Teeter, still bobbing and bowing. "If you had taken another step, Peter Rabbit, you would have stepped right on our eggs. You gave me a dreadful start."

Peter was puzzled. He showed it as he stared down at Mrs. Teeter just in front of him. "I don't see any nest or eggs or anything," said he rather testily.

Mrs. Teeter stood up and stepped aside. Then Peter saw right in a little hollow in the sand, with just a few bits of grass for a lining, four white eggs with big dark blotches on them. They looked so much like the surrounding pebbles that he never would have seen them in the world but for Mrs. Teeter. Peter hastily backed away a few steps. Mrs. Teeter slipped back on the eggs and settled herself comfortably. It suddenly struck Peter that if he hadn't seen her do it, he wouldn't have known she was there. You see she looked so much like her surroundings that he never would have noticed her at all.

"My!" he exclaimed. "I certainly would have stepped on those eggs if you hadn't warned me," said he. "I'm so thankful I didn't. I don't see how you dare lay them in the open like this."

Mrs. Teeter chuckled softly. "It's the safest place in the world, Peter," said she. "They look so much like these pebbles around here that no one sees them. The only time they are in danger is when somebody comes along, as you did, and is likely to step on them without seeing them. But that doesn't happen often."

x. Redwing and Yellow Wing.

PETER HAD come over to the Smiling Pool especially to pay his respects to Redwing the Blackbird, so as soon as he could, without being impolite, he left Mrs. Teeter sitting on her eggs, and Teeter himself bobbing and bowing in the friendliest way, and hurried over to where the bulrushes grow. In the very top of the Big Hickory-tree, a little farther along on the bank of the Smiling Pool, sat some one who at that distance appeared to be dressed all in black. He was singing as if there were nothing but joy in all the great world. "Quong-ka-reee! Quong-ka-reee! Quong-ka-reee!" he sang. Peter would have known from this song alone that it was Redwing the Blackbird, for there is no other song quite like it.

As soon as Peter appeared in sight Redwing left his high perch and flew down to light among the broken-down bulrushes. As he flew, Peter saw the beautiful red patch on the bend of each wing, from which Redwing gets his name. "No one could ever mistake him for anybody else," thought Peter, "For there isn't anybody else with such beautiful shoulder patches."

"What's the news, Peter Rabbit?" cried Redwing, coming over to sit very near Peter.

"There isn't much," replied Peter, "excepting that Teeter the Sandpiper has four eggs just a little way from here."

Redwing chuckled. "That is no news, Peter," said he. "Do you suppose that I live neighbor to Teeter and don't know where his nest is and all about his affairs? There isn't much going on around the Smiling Pool that I don't know, I can tell you that."

Peter looked a little disappointed, because there is nothing he likes better than to be the bearer of news. "I suppose," said

REDWING THE BLACKBIRD. His shoulders are brilliant red with a margin of yellow.

SPECKLES THE STARLING. He looks something like a Blackbird speckled with tiny light spots.

he politely, "that you will be building a nest pretty soon yourself, Redwing."

Redwing chuckled softly. It was a happy, contented sort of chuckle. "No, Peter," said he. "I am not going to build a nest."

"What?" exclaimed Peter, and his two long ears stood straight up with astonishment.

"No," replied Redwing, still chuckling. "I'm not going to build a nest, and if you want to know a little secret, we have four as pretty eggs as ever were laid."

Peter fairly bubbled over with interest and curiosity. "How splendid!" he cried. "Where is your nest, Redwing? I would just love to see it. I suppose it is because she is sitting on those eggs that I haven't seen Mrs. Redwing. It was very stupid of me not to guess that folks who come as early as you do would be among the first to build a home. Where is it, Redwing? Do tell me."

Redwing's eyes twinkled.

"A secret which is known by three
Full soon will not a secret be,"

said he. "It isn't that I don't trust you, Peter. I know that you wouldn't intentionally let my secret slip out. But you might do it by accident. What you don't know, you can't tell."

"That's right, Redwing. I am glad you have so much sense," said another voice, and Mrs. Redwing alighted very near to Redwing.

Peter couldn't help thinking that Old Mother Nature had been very unfair indeed in dressing Mrs. Redwing. She was, if anything, a little bit smaller than her handsome husband, and such a plain, not to say homely, little body that it was hard work to realize that she was a Blackbird at all. In the first place she wasn't black. She was dressed all over in grayish-brown with streaks of darker brown which in places were almost black. She wore no bright-colored shoulder patches. In fact, there wasn't a bright feather on her anywhere. Peter wanted to ask why it was that she was so plainly dressed, but he was too polite and decided to wait until he should see Jenny Wren. She would be sure to know. Instead, he exclaimed, "How do you do, Mrs.

Redwing? I'm ever so glad to see you. I was wondering where you were. Where did you come from?"

"Straight from my home," replied Mrs. Redwing demurely. "And if I do say it, it is the best home we've ever had."

Redwing chuckled. He was full of chuckles. You see, he had noticed how eagerly Peter was looking everywhere.

"This much I will tell you, Peter," said Redwing; "our nest is somewhere in these bulrushes, and if you can find it we won't say a word, even if you don't keep the secret."

Then Redwing chuckled again and Mrs. Redwing chuckled with him. You see, they knew that Peter doesn't like water, and that nest was hidden in a certain clump of brown, broken-down rushes, with water all around. Suddenly Redwing flew up in the air with a harsh cry. "Run, Peter! Run!" he screamed. "Here comes Reddy Fox!"

Peter didn't wait for a second warning. He knew by the sound of Redwing's voice that Redwing wasn't joking. There was just one place of safety, and that was an old hole of Grandfather Chuck's between the roots of the Big Hickory-tree. Peter didn't waste any time getting there, and he was none too soon, for Reddy was so close at his heels that he pulled some white hairs out of Peter's tail as Peter plunged headfirst down that hole. It was a lucky thing for Peter that that hole was too small for Reddy to follow and the roots prevented Reddy from digging it any bigger.

For a long time Peter sat in Grandfather Chuck's old house, wondering how soon it would be safe for him to come out. For a while he heard Mr. and Mrs. Redwing scolding sharply, and by this he knew that Reddy Fox was still about. By and by they stopped scolding, and a few minutes later he heard Redwing's happy song. "That means," thought Peter, "that Reddy Fox has gone away, but I think I'll sit here a while longer to make sure."

Now Peter was sitting right under the Big Hickory-tree. After a while he began to hear faint little sounds, little taps, and scratching sounds as of claws. They seemed to come from right over his head, but he knew that there was no one in that hole but himself. He couldn't understand it at all.

Finally Peter decided it would be safe to peek outside. Very carefully he poked his head out. Just as he did so, a little chip struck him right on the nose. Peter pulled his head back hurriedly and stared at the little chip which lay just in front of the hole. Then two or three more little chips fell. Peter knew that they must come from up in the Big Hickory-tree, and right away his curiosity was aroused. Redwing was singing so happily that Peter felt sure no danger was near, so he hopped outside and looked up to find out where those little chips had come from. Just a few feet above his head he saw a round hole in the trunk of the Big Hickory-tree. While he was looking at it, a head with a long stout bill was thrust out and in that bill were two or three little chips. Peter's heart gave a little jump of glad surprise.

"Yellow Wing!" he cried. "My goodness, how you startled me!"

The chips were dropped and the head was thrust farther out. The sides and throat were a soft reddish-tan and on each side at the beginning of the bill was a black patch. The top of the head was gray and just at the back was a little band of bright red. There was no mistaking that head. It belonged to Yellow Wing the Flicker beyond a doubt.

"Hello, Peter!" exclaimed Yellow Wing, his eyes twinkling. "What are you doing here?"

"Nothing," replied Peter, "but I want to know what you are doing. What are all those chips?"

"I'm fixing up this old house of mine," replied Yellow Wing promptly. "It wasn't quite deep enough to suit me, so I am making it a little deeper. Mrs. Yellow Wing and I haven't been able to find another house to suit us, so we have decided to live here again this year." He came wholly out and flew down on the ground near Peter. When his wings were spread, Peter saw that on the under sides they were a beautiful golden-yellow, as were the under sides of his tail feathers. Around his throat was a broad, black collar. From this, clear to his tail, were black dots. When his wings were spread, the upper part of his body just above the tail was pure white.

"My," exclaimed Peter, "you are a handsome fellow! I never realized before how handsome you are."

Yellow Wing looked pleased. Perhaps he felt a little flattered. "I am glad you think so, Peter," said he. "I am rather proud of my suit, myself. I don't know of any member of my family with whom I would change coats."

A sudden thought struck Peter. "What family do you belong to?" He asked abruptly.

"The Woodpecker family," replied Yellow Wing proudly.

YELLOW WING THE FLICKER. The bright yellow of the underside of each wing, the black crescent across his breast and his spotted underparts make him easy to identify.

XI. Drummers and Carpenters.

Peter Rabbit was so full of questions that he hardly knew which one to ask first. But Yellow Wing the Flicker didn't give him a chance to ask any. From the edge of the Green forest there came a clear, loud call of, "Pe-ok! Pe-ok! Pe-ok!"

"Excuse me, Peter, there's Mrs. Yellow Wing calling me," exclaimed Yellow Wing, and away he went. Peter noticed that as he flew he went up and down. It seemed very much as if he bounded through the air just as Peter bounds over the ground. "I would know him by the way he flies just as far as I could see him," thought Peter, as he started for home in the dear Old Briar-patch. "Somehow he doesn't seem like a Woodpecker because he is on the ground so much. I must ask Jenny Wren about him."

It was two or three days before Peter had a chance for a bit of gossip with Jenny Wren. When he did the first thing he asked was if Yellow Wing is a true Woodpecker.

"Certainly he is," replied Jenny Wren. "Of course he is. Why under the sun should you think he isn't?"

"Because it seems to me he is on the ground more than he's in the trees," retorted Peter. "I don't know any other Woodpeckers who come down on the ground at all."

"Tut, tut, tut, tut!" scolded Jenny. "Think a minute, Peter! Think a minute! Haven't you ever seen Redhead on the ground?"

Peter blinked his eyes. "Ye-e-s," he said slowly. "Come to think of it, I have. I've seen him picking up beechnuts in the fall. The Woodpeckers are a funny family. I don't understand them."

Just then a long, rolling rat-a-tat-tat rang out just over their heads. "There's another one of them," chuckled Jenny. "That's Downy, the smallest of the whole family. He certainly makes an awful racket for such a little fellow. He is a splendid drummer and he's just as good a carpenter. He made the very house I am occupying now."

Peter was sitting with his head tipped back trying to see Downy. At first he couldn't make him out. Then he caught a little movement on top of a dead limb. It was Downy's head flying back and forth as he beat his long roll. He was dressed all in black and white. On the back of his head was a little scarlet patch. He was making a tremendous racket for such a little chap, only a little bigger than one of the Sparrow family.

"Is he making a hole for a nest up there?" asked Peter eagerly.

"Gracious, Peter, what a question! What a perfectly silly question!" exclaimed Jenny Wren scornfully. "Do give us birds credit for a little common sense. If he were cutting a hole for a nest, everybody within hearing would know just where to look for it. Downy has too much sense in that little head of his to do such a silly thing as that. When he cuts a hole for a nest he doesn't make any more noise than is absolutely necessary. You don't see any chips flying, do you?"

"No-o," replied Peter slowly. "Now you speak of it, I don't. Is—is he hunting for worms in the wood?"

Jenny laughed right out. "Hardly, Peter, hardly," said she. "He's just drumming, that's all. That hollow limb makes the best kind of a drum and Downy is making the most of it. Just listen to that! There isn't a better drummer anywhere."

But Peter wasn't satisfied. Finally he ventured another question. "What's he doing it for?"

"Good land, Peter!" cried Jenny. "What do you run and jump for in the spring? What is Mr. Wren singing for over there? Downy is drumming for precisely the same reason—happiness. He can't run and jump and he can't sing, but he can drum. By the way, do you know that Downy is one of the most useful birds in the Old Orchard?"

Just then Downy flew away, but hardly had he disappeared when another drummer took his place. At first Peter thought Downy had returned until he noticed that the newcomer was just a bit bigger than Downy. Jenny Wren's sharp eyes spied him at once.

REDHEAD THE WOODPECKER. You will know him instantly by his all-red head.

DOWNY THE WOODPECKER. His smaller size and the black bars on the white outer feathers of his tail distinguish him.

"Hello!" she exclaimed. "There's Hairy. Did you ever see two cousins look more alike? If it were not that Hairy is bigger than Downy it would be hard work to tell them apart. Do you see any other difference, Peter?"

Peter stared and blinked and stared again, then slowly shook his head. "No," he confessed, "I don't."

"That shows you haven't learned to use your eyes, Peter," said Jenny rather sharply. "Look at the outside feathers of his tail; they are all white. Downy's outside tail feathers have little bars of black. Hairy is just as good a carpenter as is Downy, but for that matter I don't know of a member of the Woodpecker family who isn't a good carpenter. Where did you say Yellow Wing the Flicker is making his home this year?"

"Over in the Big Hickory-tree by the Smiling Pool," replied Peter. "I don't understand yet why Yellow Wing spends so much time on the ground."

"Ants," replied Jenny Wren. "Just ants. He's as fond of ants as is Old Mr. Toad, and that is saying a great deal. If Yellow Wing keeps on he'll become a ground bird instead of a tree bird. He gets more than half his living on the ground now. Speaking of drumming, did you ever hear Yellow Wing drum on a tin roof?"

Peter shook his head.

"Well, if there's a tin roof anywhere around, and Yellow Wing can find it, he will be perfectly happy. He certainly does love to make a noise, and tin makes the finest kind of a drum."

Just then Jenny was interrupted by the arrival, on the trunk of the very next tree to the one on which she was sitting, of a bird about the size of Sammy Jay. His whole head and neck were a beautiful, deep red. His breast was pure white, and his back was black to nearly the beginning of his tail, where it was white.

"Hello, Redhead!" exclaimed Jenny Wren. "How did you know we were talking about your family?"

"Hello, chatterbox," retorted Redhead with a twinkle in his eyes. "I didn't know you were talking about my family, but I could have guessed that you were talking about some one's family. Does your tongue ever stop, Jenny?"

Jenny Wren started to become indignant and scold, then thought better of it. "I was talking for Peter's benefit," said she, trying to look dignified, a thing quite impossible for any member of the Wren family to do. "Peter has always had the idea that true Woodpeckers never go down on the ground. I was explaining to him that Yellow Wing is a true Woodpecker, yet spends half his time on the ground."

Redhead nodded. "It's all on account of ants," said he. "I don't know of any one quite so fond of ants unless it is Old Mr. Toad. I like a few of them myself, but Yellow Wing just about lives on them when he can. You may have noticed that I go down on the ground myself once in a while. I am rather fond of beetles, and an occasional grasshopper tastes very good to me. I like a variety. Yes, sir, I certainly do like a variety—cherries, blackberries, raspberries, strawberries, grapes. In fact most kinds of fruit taste good to me, not to mention beechnuts and acorns when there is no fruit."

Jenny Wren tossed her head. "You didn't mention the eggs of some of your neighbors," said she sharply.

Redhead did his best to look innocent, but Peter noticed that he gave a guilty start and very abruptly changed the subject, and a moment later flew away.

"Is it true," asked Peter, "that Redhead does such a dreadful thing?"

Jenny bobbed her head rapidly and jerked her tail. "So I an told," said she. "I've never seen him do it, but I know others who have. They say he is no better than Sammy Jay or Blacky the Crow. But gracious, goodness! I can't sit here gossiping forever." Jenny twitched her funny little tail, snapped her bright eyes at Peter, and disappeared in her house.

CREAKER THE PURPLE GRACKLE. At a distance he appears black and is called Crow Blackbird.
THE MALE COWBIRD. You may know him by his coffee-brown head.

XII. Some Unlikely Relatives.

Having other things to attend to, or rather having other things to arouse his curiosity, Peter Rabbit did not visit the Old Orchard for several days. When he did it was to find the entire neighborhood quite upset. There was an indignation meeting in progress in and around the tree in which Chebec and his modest little wife had their home. How the tongues did clatter! Peter knew that something had happened, but though he listened with all his might he couldn't make head or tail of it.

Finally Peter managed to get the attention of Jenny Wren. "What's happened?" demanded Peter. "What's all this fuss about?"

Jenny Wren was so excited that she couldn't keep still an instant. Her sharp little eyes snapped and her tail was carried higher than ever. "It's a disgrace! It's a disgrace to the whole feathered race, and something ought to be done about it!" sputtered Jenny. "I'm ashamed to think that such a contemptible creature wears feathers! I am so!"

"But what's it all about?" demanded Peter impatiently. "Do keep still long enough to tell me. Who is this contemptible creature?"

"Sally Sly," snapped Jenny Wren. "Sally Sly the Cowbird. I hoped she wouldn't disgrace the Old Orchard this year, but she has. When Mr. and Mrs. Chebec returned from getting their breakfast this morning they found one of Sally Sly's eggs in their nest. They are terribly upset, and I don't blame them. If I were in their place I simply would throw that egg out. That's what I'd do, I'd throw that egg out!"

Peter was puzzled. He blinked his eyes and stroked his whiskers as he tried to understand what it all meant. "Who is Sally

Sly, and what did she do that for?" he finally ventured.

"For goodness' sake, Peter Rabbit, do you mean to tell me you don't know who Sally Sly is?" Then without waiting for Peter to reply, Jenny rattled on. "She's a member of the Blackbird family and she's the laziest, most good-for-nothing, sneakiest, most unfeeling and most selfish wretch I know of!" Jenny paused long enough to get her breath. "She laid that egg in Chebec's nest because she is too lazy to build a nest of her own and too selfish to take care of her own children. Do you know what will happen, Peter Rabbit? Do you know what will happen?"

Peter shook his head and confessed that he didn't. "When that egg hatches out, that young Cowbird will be about twice as big as Chebec's own children," sputtered Jenny. "He'll be so big that he'll get most of the food. He'll just rob those little Chebecs in spite of all their mother and father can do. And Chebec and his wife will be just soft-hearted enough to work themselves to skin and bone to feed the young wretch because he is an orphan and hasn't anybody to look after him. The worst of it is, Sally Sly is likely to play the same trick on others. She always chooses the nest of some one smaller than herself. She's terribly sly. No one has seen her about. She just sneaked into the Old Orchard this morning when everybody was busy, laid that egg and sneaked out again."

"Did you say that she is a member of the Blackbird family?" asked Peter.

Jenny Wren nodded vigorously. "That's what she is," said she. "Thank goodness, she isn't a member of *my* family. If she were I never would be able to hold my head up. Just listen to Goldy the Oriole over in that big elm. I don't see how he can sing like that, knowing that one of his relatives has just done such a shameful deed. It's a queer thing that there can be two members of the same family so unlike. Mrs. Goldy builds one of the most wonderful nests of any one I know, and Sally Sly is too lazy to build any. If I were in Goldy's place I—"

"Hold on!" cried Peter. "I thought you said Sally Sly is a member of the Blackbird family. I don't see what she's got to do with Goldy the Oriole."

"You don't, eh?" exclaimed Jenny. "Well, for one who pokes

into other people's affairs as you do, you don't know much. The Orioles and the Meadow Larks and the Grackles and the Bobolinks all belong to the Blackbird family. They're all related to Redwing the Blackbird, and Sally Sly the Cowbird belongs in the same family."

Peter gasped. "I—I—hadn't the least idea that any of these folks were related," stammered Peter.

"Well, they are," retorted Jenny Wren. "As I live, there's Sally Sly now!"

Peter caught a glimpse of a brownish-gray bird who reminded him somewhat of Mrs. Redwing. She was about the same size and looked very much like her. It was plain that she was trying to keep out of sight, and the instant she knew that she had been discovered she flew away in the direction of the Old Pasture. It happened that late that afternoon Peter visited the Old Pasture and saw her again. She and some of her friends were busily walking about close to the feet of the cows, where they seemed to be picking up food. One had a brown head, neck and breast; the rest of his coat was glossy black. Peter rightly guessed that this must be Mr. Cowbird. Seeing them on such good terms with the cows he understood why they are called Cowbirds.

Sure that Sally Sly had left the Old Orchard, the feathered folks settled down to their personal affairs and household cares, Jenny Wren among them. Having no one to talk to, Peter found a shady place close to the old stone wall and there sat down to think over the surprising things he had learned. Presently Goldy the Baltimore Oriole alighted in the nearest apple-tree, and it seemed to Peter that never had he seen any one more beautifully dressed. His head, neck, throat and upper part of his back were black. The lower part of his back and his breast were a beautiful deep orange color. There was a dash of orange on his shoulders, but the rest of his wings were black with an edging of white. His tail was black and orange. Peter had heard him called the Firebird, and now he understood why. His song was quite as rich and beautiful as his coat.

Shortly he was joined by Mrs. Goldy. Compared with her handsome husband she was very modestly dressed. She wore more brown than black, and where the orange color appeared it was rather dull. She wasted no time in singing. Almost instantly her sharp eyes spied a piece of string caught in the bushes almost over Peter's head. With a little cry of delight she flew down and seized it. But the string was caught, and though she tugged and pulled with all her might she couldn't get it free. Goldy saw the trouble she was having and cutting his song short, flew down to help her. Together they pulled and tugged and tugged and pulled, until they had to stop to rest and get their breath.

"We simply must have this piece of string," said Mrs. Goldy. "I've been hunting everywhere for a piece, and this is the first I've found. It is just what we need to bind our nest fast to the twigs. With this I won't have the least bit of fear that that nest will ever tear loose, no matter how hard the wind blows."

Once more they tugged and pulled and pulled and tugged until at last they got it free, and Mrs. Goldy flew away in triumph with the string in her bill. Goldy himself followed. Peter watched them fly to the top of a long, swaying branch of a big elm-tree up near Farmer Brown's house. He could see something which looked like a bag hanging there, and he knew that this must be the nest.

"Gracious!" said Peter. "They must get terribly tossed about when the wind blows. I should think their babies would be thrown out."

"Don't you worry about them," said a voice.

Peter looked up to find Welcome Robin just over him. "Mrs. Goldy makes one of the most wonderful nests I know of," continued Welcome Robin. "It is like a deep pocket made of grass, string, hair and bark, all woven together like a piece of cloth. It is so deep that it is quite safe for the babies, and they seem to enjoy being rocked by the wind. I shouldn't care for it myself because I like a solid foundation for my home, but the Goldies like it. It looks dangerous but it really is one of the safest nests I know of. Snakes and cats never get 'way up there and there are few feathered nest-robbers who can get at those eggs so deep down in the nest. Goldy is sometimes called Golden Robin. He isn't a Robin at all, but I would feel very proud if he were a member of my family. He's just as useful as he is handsome, and that's saying a great deal. He just dotes on caterpillars. There's

GOLDIE THE BALTIMORE ORIOLE. He is almost wholly black and orange and nearly the size of a Robin.

SAMMY JAY. His blue and gray coat with black and white markings makes the Blue Jay one of the easiest of all birds to recognize.

Mrs. Robin calling me. Good-by, Peter."

With this Welcome Robin flew away and Peter once more settled himself to think over all he had learned.

XIII. More of the Blackbird Family.

Peter Rabbit was dozing. Yes, sir, Peter was dozing. He didn't mean to doze, but whenever Peter sits still for a long time and tries to think, he is pretty sure to go to sleep. By and by he wakened with a start. At first he didn't know what had wakened him, but as he sat there blinking his eyes, he heard a few rich notes from the top of the nearest apple-tree. "It's Goldy the Oriole," thought Peter, and peeped out to see.

But though he looked and looked he couldn't see Goldy anywhere, but he did see a stranger. It was some one of about Goldy's size and shape. In fact he was so like Goldy, but for the color of his suit, that at first Peter almost thought Goldy had somehow changed his clothes. Of course he knew that this couldn't be, but it seemed as if it must be, for the song the stranger was singing was something like that of Goldy. The stranger's head and throat and back were black, just like Goldy's, and his wings were trimmed with white in just the same way. But the rest of his suit, instead of being the beautiful orange of which Goldy is so proud, was a beautiful chestnut color.

Peter blinked and stared very hard. "Now who can this be?" said he, speaking aloud without thinking.

"Don't you know him?" asked a sharp voice so close to Peter that it made him jump. Peter whirled around. There sat Striped Chipmunk grinning at him from the top of the old stone wall. "That's Weaver the Orchard Oriole," Striped Chipmunk rattled on. "If you don't know him you ought to, because he is one of the very nicest persons in the Old Orchard. I just love to hear him sing."

"Is—is—he related to Goldy?" asked Peter somewhat doubtfully.

"Of course," retorted Striped Chipmunk. "I shouldn't think you would have to look at him more than once to know that. He's first cousin to Goldy. There comes Mrs. Weaver. I do hope they've decided to build in the Old Orchard this year."

"I'm glad you told me who she is because I never would have guessed it," confessed Peter as he studied the newcomer. She did not look at all like Weaver. She was dressed in olive-green and dull yellow, with white markings on her wings.

Peter couldn't help thinking how much easier it must be for her than for her handsome husband to hide among the green leaves.

As he watched she flew down to the ground and picked up a long piece of grass. "They are building here, as sure as you live!" cried Striped Chipmunk. "I'm glad of that. Did you ever see their nest, Peter? Of course you haven't, because you said you had never seen them before. Their nest is a wonder, Peter. It really is. It is made almost wholly of fine grass and they weave it together in the most wonderful way."

"Do they have a hanging nest like Goldy's?" asked Peter a bit timidly.

"Not such a deep one," replied Striped Chipmunk. "They hang it between the twigs near the end of a branch, but they bind it more closely to the branch and it isn't deep enough to swing as Goldy's does."

Peter had just opened his mouth to ask another question when there was a loud sniffing sound farther up along the old stone wall. He didn't wait to hear it again. He knew that Bowser the Hound was coming.

"Good-by, Striped Chipmunk! This is no place for me," whispered Peter and started for the dear Old Briar-patch. He was in such a hurry to get there that on his way across the Green Meadows he almost ran into Jimmy Skunk before he saw him.

"What's your hurry, Peter?" demanded Jimmy

"Bowser the Hound almost found me up in the Old Orchard," panted Peter. "It's a wonder he hasn't found my tracks. I expect he will any minute. I'm glad to see you, Jimmy, but I guess I'd better be moving along."

"Don't be in such a hurry, Peter. Don't be in such a hurry," replied Jimmy, who himself never hurries. "Stop and talk a bit. That old nuisance won't bother you as long as you are with me."

Peter hesitated. He wanted to gossip, but he still felt nervous about Bowser the Hound. However, as he heard nothing of Bowser's great voice, telling all the world that he had found Peter's tracks, he decided to stop a few minutes. "What are you doing down here on the Green Meadows?" he demanded.

Jimmy grinned. "I'm looking for grasshoppers and grubs, if you must know," said he. "And I've just got a notion I may find some fresh eggs. I don't often eat them, but once in a while one tastes good."

"If you ask me, it's a funny place to be looking for eggs down here on the Green Meadows," replied Peter. "When I want a thing; I look for it where it is likely to be found."

"Just so, Peter; just so," retorted Jimmy Skunk, nodding his head with approval. "That's why I am here."

Peter looked puzzled. He was puzzled. But before he could ask another question a rollicking song caused both of them to look up. There on quivering wings in mid-air was the singer. He was dressed very much like Jimmy Skunk himself, in black and white, save that in places the white had a tinge of yellow, especially on the back of his neck. It was Bubbling Bob the Bobolink. And how he did sing! It seemed as if the notes fairly tumbled over each other.

Jimmy Skunk raised himself on his hind-legs a little to see just where Bubbling Bob dropped down in the grass. Then Jimmy began to move in that direction. Suddenly Peter understood. He remembered that Bubbling Bob's nest is always on the ground. It was his eggs that Jimmy Skunk was looking for.

"You don't happen to have seen Mrs. Bob anywhere around here, do you, Peter?" asked Jimmy, trying to speak carelessly.

"No," replied Peter. "If I had I wouldn't tell you where. You ought to be ashamed, Jimmy Skunk, to think of robbing such a beautiful singer as Bubbling Bob."

"Pooh!" retorted Jimmy. "What's the harm? If I find those eggs he and Mrs. Bob could simply build another nest and lay some more. They won't be any the worse off, and I will have had a good breakfast."

"But think of all the work they would have to do to build another nest," replied Peter.

"I should worry," retorted Jimmy Skunk. "Any one who can spend so much time singing can afford to do a little extra work."

"You're horrid, Jimmy Skunk. You're just horrid," said Peter. "I hope you won't find a single egg, so there!"

With this, Peter once more headed for the dear Old Briar-patch, while Jimmy Skunk continued toward the place where Bubbling Bob had disappeared in the long grass. Peter went only a short distance and then sat up to watch Jimmy Skunk. Just before Jimmy reached the place where Bubbling Bob had disappeared, the latter mounted into the air again, pouring out his rollicking song as if there were no room in his heart for anything but happiness. Then he saw Jimmy Skunk and became very much excited. He flew down in the grass a little farther on and then up again, and began to scold.

It looked very much as if he had gone down in the grass to warn Mrs. Bob. Evidently Jimmy thought so, for he at once headed that way. When Bubbling Bob did the same thing all over again. Peter grew anxious. He knew just how patient Jimmy Skunk could be, and he very much feared that Jimmy would find that nest. Presently he grew tired of watching and started on for the dear Old Briar-patch. Just before he reached it a brown bird, who reminded him somewhat of Mrs. Redwing and Sally Sly the Cowbird, though she was smaller, ran across the path in front of him and then flew up to the top of a last year's mullein stalk. It was Mrs. Bobolink. Peter knew her well, for he and she were very good friends.

"Oh!" cried Peter. "What are you doing here? Don't you know that Jimmy Skunk, is hunting for your nest over there? Aren't you worried to death? I would be if I were in your place."

Mrs. Bob chuckled. "Isn't he a dear? And isn't he smart?" said she, meaning Bubbling Bob, of course, and not Jimmy Skunk. "Just see him lead that black-and-white robber away."

Peter stared at her for a full minute. "Do you mean to say," said he "that your nest isn't over there at all?"

Mrs. Bob chuckled harder than ever. "Of course it isn't over there," said she.

BUBBLING BOB THE BOBOLINK. He is dressed in black and yellowish white.

"Then where is it?" demanded Peter.

"That's telling," replied Mrs. Bob. "It isn't over there, and it isn't anywhere near there. But where it is is Bob's secret and mine, and we mean to keep it. Now I must go get something to eat," and with a hasty farewell Mrs. Bobolink flew over to the other side of the dear Old Briar-patch.

Peter remembered that he had seen Mrs. Bob running along the ground before she flew up to the old mullein stalk. He went back to the spot where he had first seen her and hunted all around in the grass, but without success. You see, Mrs. Bobolink had been quite as clever in fooling Peter as Bubbling Bob had been in fooling Jimmy Skunk.

XIV. Bob White and Carol the Meadow Lark.

"Bob—Bob White! Bob—Bob White! Bob—Bob White!" clear and sweet, that call floated over to the dear Old Briar-patch until Peter could stand it no longer. He felt that he just had to go over and pay an early morning call on one of his very best friends, who at this season of the year delights in whistling his own name—Bob White.

"I suppose," muttered Peter, "that Bob White has got a nest. I wish he would show it to me. He's terribly secretive about it. Last year I hunted for his nest until my feet were sore, but it wasn't the least bit of use. Then one morning I met Mrs. Bob White with fifteen babies out for a walk. How she could hide a nest with fifteen eggs in it is more than I can understand."

Peter left the Old Briar-patch and started off over the Green Meadows towards the Old Pasture. As he drew near the fence between the Green Meadows and the Old Pasture he saw Bob White sitting on one of the posts, whistling with all his might. On another post near him sat another bird very near the size of Welcome Robin. He also was telling all the world of his happiness. It was Carol the Meadow Lark.

Peter was so intent watching these two friends of his that he took no heed to his footsteps. Suddenly there was a whirr from almost under his very nose and he stopped short, so startled that he almost squealed right out. In a second he recognized Mrs. Meadow Lark. He watched her fly over to where Carol was singing. Her stout little wings moved swiftly for a moment or two, then she sailed on without moving them at all. Then they fluttered rapidly again until she was flying fast enough to once more sail on them outstretched. The white outer feathers of her tail showed clearly and reminded Peter of the tail of Sweetvoice the Vesper Sparrow, only of course it was ever so much bigger.

Peter sat still until Mrs. Meadow Lark had alighted on the fence near Carol. Then he prepared to hurry on, for he was anxious for a bit of gossip with these good friends of his. But just before he did this he just happened to glance down and there, almost at his very feet, he caught sight of something that made him squeal right out. It was a nest with four of the prettiest eggs Peter ever had seen. They were white with brown spots all over them. Had it not been for the eggs he never would have seen that nest, never in the world. It was made of dry, brown grass and was cunningly hidden is a little clump of dead grass which fell over it so as to almost completely hide it. But the thing that surprised Peter most was the clever way in which the approach to it was hidden. It was by means of a regular little tunnel of grass.

"Oh!" cried Peter, and his eyes sparkled with pleasure. "This must be the nest of Mrs. Meadow Lark. No wonder I have never been able to find it, when I have looked for it. It is just luck and nothing else that I have found it this time. I think it is perfectly wonderful that Mrs. Meadow Lark can hide her home in such a way. I do hope Jimmy Skunk isn't anywhere around."

Peter sat up straight and anxiously looked this way and that way. Jimmy Skunk was nowhere to be seen and Peter gave a little sigh of relief. Very carefully he walked around that nest and its little tunnel, then hurried over toward the fence as fast as he could go.

"It's perfectly beautiful, Carol!" he cried, just as soon as he was near enough. "And I won't tell a single soul!"

"I hope not. I certainly hope not," cried Mrs. Meadow Lark in an anxious tone. "I never would have another single easy minute if I thought you would tell a living soul about my nest. Promise that you won't, Peter. Cross your heart and promise that you won't."

Peter promptly crossed his heart and promised that he wouldn't tell a single soul. Mrs. Meadow Lark seemed to feel better. Right away she flew back and Peter turned to watch her. He saw her disappear in the grass, but it wasn't where he had found the nest. Peter waited a few minutes, thinking that he would see her rise into the air again and fly over to the nest. But he waited in vain. Then with a puzzled look on his face, he turned to look up at Carol.

Carol's eyes twinkled. "I know what you're thinking, Peter," he chuckled. "You are thinking that it is funny Mrs. Meadow Lark didn't go straight back to our nest when she seemed so anxious about it. I would have you to know that she is too clever to do anything so foolish as that. She knows well enough that somebody might see her and so find our secret. She has walked there from the place where you saw her disappear in the grass. That is the way we always do when we go to our nest. One never can be too careful these days."

Then Carol began to pour out his happiness once more, quite as if nothing had interrupted his song.

Somehow Peter never before had realized how handsome Carol the Meadow Lark was. As he faced Peter, the latter saw a beautiful yellow throat and waistcoat, with a broad black crescent on his breast. There was a yellow line above each eye. His back was of brown with black markings. His sides were whitish, with spats and streaks of black. The outer edges of his tail were white. Altogether he was really handsome, far handsomer than one would suspect, seeing him at a distance.

Having found out Carol's secret, Peter was doubly anxious to find Bob White's home, so he hurried over to the post where Bob was whistling with all his might. "Bob!" cried Peter. "I've just found Carol's nest and I've promised to keep it a secret. Won't you show me your nest, too, if I'll promise to keep *that* a secret?"

Rob threw back his head and laughed joyously. "You ought to know, Peter, by this time," said he, "that there are secrets never to be told to anybody. My nest is one of these. If you find it, all right; but I wouldn't show it to my very best friend, and I guess I haven't any better friend than you, Peter." Then from sheer happiness he whistled, "—Bob White! Bob—Bob White!" with all his might.

Peter was disappointed and a little put out. "I guess," said he, "I could find it if I wanted to. I guess it isn't any better hidden than Mrs. Meadow Lark's, and I found that. Some folks aren't

CAROL THE MEADOW LARK. You will know him by the black crescent on his yellow breast, and the white outer feathers of his rather short tail when he flies.

as smart as they think they are."

Bob White, who is sometimes called Quail and sometimes called Partridge, and who is neither, chuckled heartily. "Go ahead, old Mr. Curiosity, go ahead and hunt all you please," said he. "It's funny to me how some folks think themselves smart when the truth is they simply have been lucky. You know well enough that you just happened to find Carol's nest. If you happen to find mine, I won't have a word to say."

Bob White took a long breath, tipped his head back until his bill was pointing right up in the blue, blue sky, and with all his might whistled his name, "Bob—Bob White! Bob—Bob White!"

As Peter looked at him it came over him that Bob White was the plumpest bird of his acquaintance. He was so plump that his body seemed almost round. The shortness of his tail added to this effect, for Bob has a very short tail. The upper part of his coat was a handsome reddish-brown with dark streaks and light edgings. His sides and the upper part of his breast were of the same handsome reddish-brown, while underneath he was whitish with little bars of black. His throat was white, and above each eye was a broad white stripe. His white throat was bordered with black, and a band of black divided the throat from the white line above each eye. The top of his head was mixed black and brown. Altogether he was a handsome little fellow in a modest way.

Suddenly Bob White stopped whistling and looked down at Peter with a twinkle in his eye. "Why don't you go hunt for that nest, Peter?" said he.

"I'm going," replied Peter rather shortly, for he knew that Bob knew that he hadn't the least idea where to look. It might be somewhere on the Green Meadows or it might be in the Old Pasture; Bob hadn't given the least hint. Peter had a feeling that the nest wasn't far away and that it was on the Green Meadows, so he began to hunt, running aimlessly this way and that way, all the time feeling very foolish, for of course he knew that Bob White was watching him and chuckling down inside.

It was very warm down there on the Green Meadows, and Peter grew hot and tired. He decided to run up in the Old Pasture in the shade of an old bramble-tangle there. Just the other side of the fence was a path made by the cows and often used by Farmer Brown's boy and Reddy Fox and others who visited the Old Pasture. Along this Peter scampered, lipperty-lipperty-lip, on his way to the bramble-tangle. He didn't look either to right or left. It didn't occur to him that there would be any use at all, for of course no one would build a nest near a path where people passed to and fro every day.

And so it was that in his happy-go-lucky way Peter scampered right past a clump of tall weeds close beside the path without the least suspicion that cleverly hidden in it was the very thing he was looking for. With laughter in her eyes, shrewd little Mrs. Bob White, with sixteen white eggs under her, watched him pass. She had chosen that very place for her nest because she knew that it was the last place anyone would expect to find it. The very fact that it seemed the most dangerous place she could have chosen made it the safest.

XV. A Swallow and One Who Isn't.

JOHNNY AND Polly Chuck had made their home between the roots of an old apple-tree in the far corner of the Old Orchard. You know they have their bedroom way down in the ground, and it is reached by a long hall. They had dug their home between the roots of that old apple-tree because they had discovered that there was just room enough between those spreading roots for them to pass in and out, and there wasn't room to dig the entrance any larger. So they felt quite safe from Reddy Fox; and Bowser the Hound, either of whom would have delighted to dig them out but for those roots.

Right in front of their doorway was a very nice doorstep of shining sand where Johnny Chuck delighted to sit when he had a full stomach and nothing else to do. Johnny's nearest neighbors had made their home only about five feet above Johnny's head when he sat up on his doorstep. They were Skimmer the Tree Swallow and his trim little wife, and the doorway of their home was a little round hole in the trunk of that apple-tree, a hole which had been cut some years before by one of the Woodpeckers.

Johnny and Skimmer were the best of friends. Johnny used to delight in watching Skimmer dart out from beneath the branches of the trees and wheel and turn and glide, now sometimes high in the blue, blue sky, and again just skimming the tops of the grass, on wings which seemed never to tire. But he liked still better the bits of gossip when Skimmer would sit in his doorway and chat about his neighbors of the Old Orchard and his adventures out in the Great World during his long journeys to and from the far-away South.

To Johnny Chuck's way of thinking, there was no one quite

so trim and neat appearing as Skimmer with his snowy white breast and blue-green back and wings. Two things Johnny always used to wonder at, Skimmer's small bill and short legs. Finally he ventured to ask Skimmer about them.

"Gracious, Johnny!" exclaimed Skimmer. "I wouldn't have a big bill for anything. I wouldn't know what to do with it; it would be in the way. You see, I get nearly all my food in the air when I am flying, mosquitoes and flies and all sorts of small insects with wings. I don't have to pick them off trees and bushes or from the ground and so I don't need any more of a bill than I have. It's the same way with my legs. Have you ever seen me walking on the ground?"

Johnny thought a moment. "No," said he, "now you speak of it, I never have."

"And have you ever seen me hopping about in the branches of a tree?" persisted Skimmer.

Again Johnny Chuck admitted that he never had.

"The only use I have for feet," continued Skimmer, "is for perching while I rest. I don't need long legs for walking or hopping about, so Mother Nature has made my legs very short. You see I spend most of my time in the air."

"I suppose it's the same with your cousin; Sooty the Chimney Swallow," said Johnny.

"That shows just how much some people know!" twittered Skimmer indignantly. "The idea of calling Sooty a Swallow! The very idea! I'd leave you to know, Johnny Chuck, that Sooty isn't even related to me. He's a Swift, and not a Swallow."

"He looks like a Swallow," protested Johnny Chuck.

"He doesn't either. You just think he does because he happens to spend most of his time in the air the way we Swallows do," sputtered Skimmer. "The Swallow family never would admit such a homely looking fellow as he is as a member.

"Tut, tut, tut, tut! I do believe Skimmer is jealous," cried Jenny Wren, who had happened along just in time to hear Skimmer's last remarks.

"Nothing of the sort," declared Skimmer, growing still more indignant. "I'd like to know what there is about Sooty the Chimney Swift that could possibly make a Swallow jealous."

SKIMMER THE TREE SWALLOW. When you see a Swallow with pure white breast and blue-green back it is Skinner.

FORKTAIL THE BARN SWALLOW. His long forked tail is all you need to see to know him.

Jenny Wren cocked her tail up in that saucy way of hers and winked at Johnny Chuck. "The way he can fly," said she softly.

"The way he can fly!" sputtered Skimmer, "The way he can fly! Why, there never was a day in his life that he could fly like a Swallow. There isn't any one more graceful on the wing than I am, if I do say so. And there isn't any one more ungraceful than Sooty."

Just then there was a shrill chatter overhead and all looked up to see Sooty the Chimney Swift racing through the sky as if having the very best time in the world. His wings would beat furiously and then he would glide very much as you or I would on skates. It was quite true that he wasn't graceful. But he could twist and turn and cut up all sorts of antics, such as Skimmer never dreamed of doing.

"He can use first one wing and then the other, while you have to use both wings at once," persisted Jenny Wren. "You couldn't, to save your life, go straight down into a chimney, and you know it, Skimmer. He can do things with his wings which you can't do, nor any other bird."

"That may be true, but just the same I'm not the least teeny weeny bit jealous of him," said Skimmer, and darted away to get beyond the reach of Jenny's sharp tongue.

"Is it really true that he and Sooty are not related?" asked Johnny Chuck, as they watched Skimmer cutting airy circles high up in the sky.

Jenny nodded. "It's quite true, Johnny," said she. "Sooty belongs to another family altogether. He's a funny fellow. Did you ever in your life see such narrow wings? And his tail is hardly worth calling a tail."

Johnny Chuck laughed. "Way up there in the air he looks almost alike at both ends," said he. "Is he all black?"

"He isn't black at all," declared Jenny. "He is sooty-brown, rather grayish on the throat and breast. Speaking of that tail of his, the feathers end in little, sharp, stiff points. He uses them in the same way that Downy the Woodpecker uses his tail feathers when he braces himself with them on the trunk of a tree."

"But I've never seen Sooty on the trunk of a tree," protested Johnny Chuck. "In fact, I've never seen him anywhere but in the air."

"And you never will," snapped Jenny. "The only place he ever alights is inside a chimney or inside a hollow tree. There he clings to the side just as Downy the Woodpecker clings to the trunk of a tree."

Johnny looked as if he didn't quite believe this. "If that's the case where does he nest?" he demanded. "And where does he sleep?"

"In a chimney, stupid. In a chimney, of course," retorted Jenny Wren. "He fastens his nest right to the inside of a chimney. He makes a regular little basket of twigs and fastens it to the side of the chimney."

"Are you trying to stuff me with nonsense?" asked Johnny Chuck indignantly. "How can he fasten his nest to the side of a chimney unless there's a little shelf to put it on? And if he never alights, how does he get the little sticks to make a nest of? I'd just like to know how you expect me to believe any such story as that."

Jenny Wren's sharp little eyes snapped. "If you half used your eyes you wouldn't have to ask me how he gets those little sticks," she sputtered. "If you had watched him when he was flying close to the tree tops you would have seen him clutch little dead twigs in his claws and snap them off without stopping. That's the way he gets his little sticks, Mr. Smarty, He fastens them together with a sticky substance he has in his mouth, and he fastens the nest to the side of the chimney in the same way. You can believe it or not, but it's so."

"I believe it, Jenny, I believe it," replied Johnny Chuck very humbly. "If you please, Jenny, does Sooty get all his food in the air too?"

"Of course," replied Jenny tartly. "He eats nothing but insects, and he catches them flying. Now I must get back to my duties at home."

"Just tell me one more thing," cried Johnny Chuck hastily. "Hasn't Sooty any near relatives as most birds have?"

"He hasn't any one nearer than some sort of second cousins, Boomer the Nighthawk, Whippoorwill, and Hummer the Hummingbird."

"What?" cried Johnny Chuck, quite as if he couldn't believe he had heard aright. "Did you say Hummer the Hummingbird?" But he got no reply, for Jenny Wren was already beyond hearing.

BOOMER THE NIGHTHAWK. Look for him in the air late in the afternoon.

XVI. A ROBBER IN THE OLD ORCHARD.

"I DON'T believe it," muttered Johnny Chuck out loud. "I don't believe Jenny Wren knows what she's talking about."

"What is it Jenny Wren has said that you don't believe?" demanded Skimmer the Tree Swallow, as he once more settled himself in his doorway.

"She said that Hummer the Hummingbird is a sort of second cousin to Sooty the Chimney Swift," replied Johnny Chuck.

"Well, it's so, if you don't believe it," declared Skimmer. "I don't see that that is any harder to believe than that you are cousin to Striped Chipmunk and Happy Jack the Gray Squirrel. To look at you no one would ever think you are a member of the Squirrel family, but you must admit that you are."

Johnny Chuck nodded his head thoughtfully. "Yes," said he, "I am, even if I don't look it. This is a funny world, isn't it? You can't always tell by a person's looks who he may be related to. Now that I've found out that Sooty isn't related to you and is related to Hummer, I'll never dare guess again about anybody's relatives. I always supposed Twitter the Martin to be a relative of yours, but now that I've learned that Sooty isn't, I suspect that Twitter isn't either."

"Oh, yes, he is," replied Skimmer promptly. "He's the largest of the Swallow family, and we all feel very proud of him. Everybody loves him."

"Is he as black as he looks, flying round up in the air?" asked Johnny Chuck. "He never comes down here as you do where a fellow can get a good look at him."

"Yes," replied Skimmer, "he dresses all in black, but it is a beautiful blue-black, and when the sun shines on his back it seems to be almost purple. That is why some folks call him the Purple Martin. He is one of the most social fellows I know of. I like a home by myself, such as I've got here, but Twitter loves company. He likes to live in an apartment house with a lot of his own kind. That is why he always looks for one of those houses with a lot of rooms in it, such as Farmer Brown's boy has put up on the top of that tall pole out in his back yard. He pays for all the trouble Farmer Brown's boy took to put that house up. If there is anybody who catches more flies and winged insects than Twitter, I don't know who it is."

"How about me?" demanded a new voice, as a graceful form skimmed over Johnny Chuck's head, and turning like a flash, came back. It was Forktail the Barn Swallow, the handsomest and one of the most graceful of all the Swallow family. He passed so close to Johnny that the latter had a splendid chance to see and admire his glistening steel-blue back and the beautiful chestnut-brown of his forehead and throat with its narrow black collar, and the brown to buff color of his under parts. But the thing that was most striking about him was his tail, which was so deeply forked as to seem almost like two tails.

"I would know him as far as I could see him just by his tail alone," exclaimed Johnny. "I don't know of any other tail at all like it."

"There isn't any other like it," declared Skimmer. "If Twitter the Martin is the largest of our family, Forktail is the handsomest."

"How about my usefulness?" demanded Forktail, as he came skimming past again. "Cousin Twitter certainly does catch a lot of flies and insects but I'm willing to go against him any day to see who can catch the most."

With this he darted away. Watching him they saw him alight on the top of Farmer Brown's barn. "It's funny," remarked Johnny Chuck, "but as long as I've known Forktail, and I've known him ever since I was big enough to know anybody, I've never found out how he builds his nest. I've seen him skimming over the Green Meadows times without number, and often he comes here to the Old Orchard as he did just now, but I've never seen him stop anywhere except over on that barn."

"That's where he nests," chuckled Skimmer.

"What?" cried Johnny Chuck. "Do you mean to say he nests on Farmer Brown's barn?"

"No," replied Skimmer. "He nests in it. That's why he is called the Barn Swallow, and why you never have seen his nest. If you'll just go over to Farmer Brown's barn and look up in the roof, you'll see Forktail's nest there somewhere."

"Me go over to Farmer Brown's barn!" exclaimed Johnny Chuck. "Do you think I'm crazy?"

Skimmer chuckled. "Forktail isn't crazy," said he, "and he goes in and out of that barn all day long. I must say I wouldn't care to build in such a place myself, but he seems to like it. There's one thing about it, his home is warm and dry and comfortable, no matter what the weather is. I wouldn't trade with him, though. No, sir, I wouldn't trade with him for anything. Give me a hollow in a tree well lined with feathers to a nest made of mud and straw, even if it is feather-lined."

"Do you mean that such a neat-looking, handsome fellow as Forktail uses mud in his nest?" cried Johnny.

Skimmer bobbed his head. "He does just that," said he. "He's something like Welcome Robin in this respect. I—"

But Johnny Chuck never knew what Skimmer was going to say next, for Skimmer happened at that instant to glance up. For an instant he sat motionless with horror, then with a shriek he darted out into the air. At the sound of that shriek Mrs. Skimmer, who all the time had been sitting on her eggs inside the hollow of the tree, darted out of her doorway, also shrieking. For a moment Johnny Chuck couldn't imagine what could be the trouble. Then a slight rustling drew his eyes to a crotch in the tree a little above the doorway of Skimmer's home. There, partly coiled around a branch, with head swaying to and fro, eyes glittering and forked tongue darting out and in, as he tried to look down into Skimmer's nest, was Mr. Blacksnake.

It seemed to Johnny as if in a minute every bird in the Old Orchard had arrived on the scene. Such a shrieking and screaming as there was! First one and then another would dart at Mr. Blacksnake, only to lose courage at the last second and turn aside. Poor Skimmer and his little wife were frantic. They did their utmost to distract Mr. Blacksnake's attention, darting almost into his very face and then away again before he could strike. But Mr. Blacksnake knew that they were powerless to hurt him, and he knew that there were eggs in that nest. There is nothing he loves better than eggs unless it is a meal of baby birds. Beyond hissing angrily two or three times he paid no attention to Skimmer or his friends, but continued to creep nearer the entrance to that nest.

At last he reached a position where he could put his head in the doorway. As he did so, Skimmer and Mrs. Skimmer each gave a little cry of hopelessness and despair. But no sooner had his head disappeared in the hole in the old apple-tree than Scrapper the Kingbird struck him savagely. Instantly Mr. Blacksnake withdrew his head, hissing fiercely, and struck savagely at the birds nearest him. Several times the same thing happened. No sooner would his head disappear in that hole than Scrapper or one or the other of Skimmer's friends, braver than the rest, would dart in and peck at him viciously, and all the time all the birds were screaming as only excited feathered folk can. Johnny Chuck was quite as excited as his feathered friends, and so intent watching the hated black robber that he had eyes for nothing else. Suddenly he heard a step just behind him. He turned his head and then frantically dived head first down into his hole. He had looked right up into the eyes of Farmer Brown's boy!

"Ha, ha!" cried Farmer Brown's boy, "I thought as much!" And with a long switch he struck Mr. Blacksnake just as the latter had put his head in that doorway, resolved to get those eggs this time. But when he felt that switch and heard the voice of Farmer Brown's boy he changed his mind in a flash. He simply let go his hold on that tree and dropped. The instant he touched the ground he was off like a shot for the safety of the old stone wall, Farmer Brown's boy after him. Farmer Brown's boy didn't intend to kill Mr. Blacksnake, but he did want to give him such a fright that he wouldn't visit the Old Orchard again in a hurry, and this he quite succeeded in doing.

No sooner had Mr. Blacksnake disappeared than all the birds set up such a rejoicing that you would have thought they, and not Farmer Brown's boy, had saved the eggs of Mr. and Mrs. Skimmer. Listening to them, Johnny Chuck just had to smile.

XVII. More Robbers.

By the sounds of rejoicing among the feathered folks of the Old Orchard Johnny Chuck knew that it was quite safe for him to come out. He was eager to tell Skimmer the Tree Swallow how glad he was that Mr. Blacksnake had been driven away before he could get Skimmer's eggs. As he poked his head out of his doorway he became aware that something was still wrong in the Old Orchard. Into the glad chorus there broke a note of distress and sorrow. Johnny instantly recognized the voices of Welcome Robin and Mrs. Robin. There is not one among his feathered neighbors who can so express worry and sorrow as can the Robins.

Johnny was just in time to see all the birds hurrying over to that part of the Old Orchard where the Robins had built their home. The rejoicing suddenly gave way to cries of indignation and anger, and Johnny caught the words, "Robber! Thief! Wretch!" It appeared that there was just as much excitement over there as there had been when Mr. Blacksnake had been discovered trying to rob Skimmer and Mrs. Skimmer. It couldn't be Mr. Blacksnake again, because Farmer Brown's boy had chased him in quite another direction.

"What is it now?" asked Johnny of Skimmer, who was still excitedly discussing with Mrs. Skimmer their recent fright.

"I don't know, but I'm going to find out," replied Skimmer and darted away.

Johnny Chuck waited patiently. The excitement among the birds seemed to increase, and the chattering and angry cries grew louder. Only the voices of Welcome and Mrs. Robin were not angry. They were mournful, as if Welcome and Mrs. Robin were heartbroken. Presently Skimmer came back to tell Mrs. Skimmer the news.

"The Robins have lost their eggs!" he cried excitedly. "All four have been broken and eaten. Mrs. Robin left them to come over here to help drive away Mr. Blacksnake, and while she was here some one ate those eggs. Nobody knows who it could have been, because all the birds of the Old Orchard were over here at that time. It might have been Chatterer the Red Squirrel, or it might have been Sammy Jay, or it might have been Creaker the Grackle, or it might have been Blacky the Crow. Whoever it was just took that chance to sneak over there and rob that nest when there was no one to see him."

Just then from over towards the Green Forest sounded a mocking "Caw, caw, caw!" Instantly the noise in the Old Orchard ceased for a moment. Then it broke out afresh. There wasn't a doubt now in any one's mind. Blacky the Crow was the robber. How those tongues did go! There was nothing too bad to say about Blacky. And such dreadful things as those birds promised to do to Blacky the Crow if ever they should catch him in the Old Orchard.

"Caw, caw, caw!" shouted Blacky from the distance, and his voice sounded very much as if he thought he had done something very smart. It was quite clear that at least he was not sorry for what he had done.

All the birds were so excited and so angry, as they gathered around Welcome and Mrs. Robin trying to comfort them, that it was some time before their indignation meeting broke up and they returned to their own homes and duties. Almost at once there was another cry of distress. Mr. and Mrs. Chebec had been robbed of their eggs! While they had been attending the indignation meeting at the home of the Robins, a thief had taken the chance to steal their eggs and get away.

Of course right away all the birds hurried over to sympathize with the Chebecs and to repeat against the unknown thief all the threats they had made against Blacky the Crow. They knew it couldn't have been Blacky this time because they had heard Blacky cawing over on the edge of the Green Forest. In the midst of the excited discussion as to who the thief was, Weaver the

Orchard Oriole spied a blue and white feather on the ground just below Chebec's nest.

"It was Sammy Jay! There is no doubt about it, it was Sammy Jay!" he cried.

At the sight of that telltale feather all the birds knew that Weaver was right, and led by Scrapper the Kingbird they began a noisy search of the Old Orchard for the sly robber. But Sammy wasn't to be found, and they soon gave up the search, none daring to stay longer away from his own home lest something should happen there. Welcome and Mrs. Robin continued to cry mournfully, but little Mr. and Mrs. Chebec bore their trouble almost silently.

"There is one thing about it," said Mr. Chebec to his sorrowful little wife, "that egg of Sally Sly's went with the rest, and we won't have to raise that bothersome orphan."

"That's true," said she. "There is no use crying over what can't be helped. It is a waste of time to sit around crying. Come on, Chebec, let's look for a place to build another nest. Next time I won't leave the eggs unwatched for a minute."

Meanwhile Jenny Wren's tongue was fairly flying as she chattered to Peter Rabbit, who had come up in the midst of the excitement and of course had to know all about it.

"Blacky the Crow has a heart as black as his coat, and his cousin Sammy Jay isn't much better," declared Jenny. "They belong to a family of robbers."

"Wait a minute," cried Peter. "Do you mean to say that Blacky the Crow and Sammy Jay are cousins?"

"For goodness' sake, Peter!" exclaimed Jenny, "do you mean to say that you don't know that? Of course they're cousins. They don't look much alike, but they belong to the same family. I would expect almost anything bad of any one as black as Blacky the Crow. But how such a handsome fellow as Sammy Jay can do such dreadful things I don't understand. He isn't as bad as Blacky, because he does do a lot of good. He destroys a lot of caterpillars and other pests.

"There are no sharper eyes anywhere than those of Sammy Jay, and I'll have to say this for him, that whenever he discovers any danger he always gives us warning. He has saved the lives of a good many of us feathered folks in this way. If it wasn't for this habit of stealing our eggs I wouldn't have a word to say against him, but at that, he isn't as bad as Blacky the Crow. They say Blacky does some good by destroying white grubs and some other harmful pests, but he's a regular cannibal, for he is just as fond of young birds as he is of eggs, and the harm he does in this way is more than the good he does in other ways. He's bold, black, and bad, if you ask me."

Remembering her household duties, Jenny Wren disappeared inside her house in her usual abrupt fashion. Peter hung around for a while but finding no one who would take the time to talk to him he suddenly decided to go over to the Green Forest to look for some of his friends there. He had gone but a little way in the Green Forest when he caught a glimpse of a blue form stealing away through the trees. He knew it in an instant, for there is no one with such a coat but Sammy Jay. Peter glanced up in the tree from which Sammy had flown and there he saw a nest in a crotch halfway up. "I wonder," thought Peter, "if Sammy was stealing eggs there, or if that is his own nest." Then he started after Sammy as fast as he could go, lipperty-lipperty-lip. As he ran he happened to look back and was just in time to see Mrs. Jay slip on to the nest. Then Peter knew that he had discovered Sammy's home. He chuckled as he ran.

"I've found out your secret, Sammy Jay!" cried Peter when at last he caught up with Sammy.

"Then I hope you'll be gentleman enough to keep it," grumbled Sammy, looking not at all pleased.

"Certainly," replied Peter with dignity. "I wouldn't think of telling any one. My, what a handsome fellow you are, Sammy."

Sammy looked pleased. He is a little bit vain, is Sammy Jay. There is no denying that he is handsome. He is just a bit bigger than Welcome Robin. His back is grayish-blue. His tail is a bright blue crossed with little black bars and edged with white. His wings are blue with white and black bars. His throat and breast are a soft grayish-white, and he wears a collar of black. On his head he wears a pointed cap, a very convenient cap, for at times he draws it down so that it is not pointed at all.

"Why did you steal Mrs. Chebec's eggs?" demanded Peter

abruptly.

Sammy didn't look the least bit put out. "Because I like eggs," he replied promptly. "If people will leave their eggs unguarded they must expect to lose them. How did you know I took those eggs?"

"Never mind, Sammy; never mind. A little bird told me," retorted Peter mischievously.

Sammy opened his mouth for a sharp reply, but instead he uttered a cry of warning. "Run, Peter! Run! Here comes Reddy Fox!" he cried.

Peter dived headlong under a great pile of brush. There he was quite safe. While he waited for Reddy Fox to go away he thought about Sammy Jay. "It's funny," he mused, "how so much good and so much bad can be mixed together. Sammy Jay stole Chebec's eggs, and then he saved my life. I just know he would have done as much for Mr. and Mrs. Chebec, or for any other feathered neighbor. He can only steal eggs for a little while in the spring. I guess on the whole he does more good than harm. I'm going to think so anyway."

Peter was quite right. Sammy Jay does do more good than harm.

XVIII. Some Homes in the Green Forest.

Reddy Fox wasted very little time waiting for Peter Rabbit to come out from under that pile of brush where he had hidden at Sammy Jay's warning. After making some terrible threats just to try to frighten Peter, he trotted away to look for some Mice. Peter didn't mind those threats at all. He was used to them. He knew that he was safe where he was, and all he had to do was to stay there until Reddy should be so far away that it would be safe to come out.

Just to pass away the time Peter took a little nap. When he awoke he sat for a few minutes trying to make up his mind where to go and what to do next. From 'way over in the direction of the Old Pasture the voice of Blacky the Crow reached him. Peter pricked up his ears, then chuckled.

"Reddy Fox has gone back to the Old Pasture and Blacky has discovered him there," he thought happily. You see, he understood what Blacky was saying. To you or me Blacky would have been saying simply, "Caw! Caw!" But to all the little people of the Green Forest and Green Meadows within hearing he was shouting, "Fox! Fox!"

"I wonder," thought Peter, "where Blacky is nesting this year. Last year his nest was in a tall pine-tree not far from the edge of the Green Forest. I believe I'll run over there and see if he has a new nest near the old one."

So Peter scampered over to the tall pine in which was Blacky's old nest. As he sat with his head tipped back, staring up at it, it struck him that that nest didn't look so old, after all. In fact, it looked as if it had recently been fixed up quite like new. He was wondering about this and trying to guess what it meant, when

REDTAIL THE HAWK. This is one of our largest hawks and may be recognized by the chestnut red of his tail.

Blacky himself alighted close to the edge of it.

There was something in his bill, though what it was Peter couldn't see. Almost at once a black head appeared above the edge of the nest and a black bill seized the thing which Blacky had brought. Then the head disappeared and Blacky silently flew away.

"As sure as I live," thought Peter, "that was Mrs. Blacky, and Blacky brought her some food so that she would not have to leave those eggs she must have up there. He may be the black-hearted robber every one says he is, but he certainly is a good husband. He's a better husband than some others I know, of whom nothing but good is said. It just goes to show that there is some good in the very worst folks. Blacky is a sly old rascal. Usually he is as noisy as any one I know, but he came and went without making a sound. Now I think of it, I haven't once heard his voice near here this spring. I guess if Farmer Brown's boy could find this nest he would get even with Blacky for pulling up his corn. I know a lot of clever people, but no one quite so clever as Blacky the Crow. With all his badness I can't help liking him."

Twice, while Peter watched, Blacky returned with food for Mrs. Blacky. Then, tired of keeping still so long, Peter decided to run over to a certain place farther in the Green Forest which was seldom visited by any one. It was a place Peter usually kept away from. It was pure curiosity which led him to go there now. The discovery that Blacky the Crow was using his old nest had reminded Peter that Redtail the Hawk uses his old nest year after year, and he wanted to find out if Redtail had come back to it this year.

Halfway over to that lonesome place in the Green Forest a trim little bird flew up from the ground, hopped from branch to branch of a tree, walked along a limb, then from pure happiness threw back his head and cried, "Teacher, teacher, teacher, teacher, teacher!" each time a little louder than before. It was Teacher the Oven Bird.

In his delight at seeing this old friend, Peter quite forgot Redtail the Hawk. "Oh, Teacher!" cried Peter. "I'm so glad to see you again!"

Teacher stopped singing and looked down at Peter. "If you are so glad why haven't you been over to see me before?" he demanded. "I've been here for some time."

Peter looked a little foolish. "The truth is, Teacher," said he very humbly, "I have been visiting the Old Orchard so much and learning so many things that this is the first chance I have had to come 'way over here in the Green Forest. You see, I have been learning a lot of things about you feathered folks, things I hadn't even guessed. There is something I wish you'd tell me, Teacher; will you?"

"That depends on what it is," replied Teacher, eyeing Peter a little suspiciously.

"It is why you are called Oven Bird," said Peter.

"Is that all?" asked Teacher. Then without waiting for a reply he added, "It is because of the way Mrs. Teacher and I build our nest. Some people think it is like an oven and so they call us Oven Birds. I think that is a silly name myself, quite as silly as Golden Crowned Thrush, which is what some people call me. I'm not a Thrush. I'm not even related to the Thrush family. I'm a Warbler, a Wood Warbler."

"I suppose," said Peter, looking at Teacher thoughtfully, "they've given you that name because you are dressed something like the Thrushes. That olive-green coat, and white waistcoat all streaked and spotted with black, certainly does remind me of the Thrush family. If you were not so much smaller than any of the Thrushes I should almost think you were one myself. Why, you are not very much bigger than Chippy the Chipping Sparrow, only you've got longer legs. I suppose that's because you spend so much time on the ground. I think that just Teacher is the best name for you. No one who has once heard you could ever mistake you for any one else. By the way, Teacher, where did you say your nest is?"

"I didn't say," retorted Teacher. "What's more, I'm not going to say."

"Won't you at least tell me if it is in a tree?" begged Peter.

Teacher's eyes twinkled. "I guess it won't do any harm to tell you that much," said he. "No, it isn't in a tree. It is on the ground and, if I do say it, it is as well hidden a nest as anybody can build. Oh, Peter, watch your step! Watch your step!" Teacher fairly shrieked this warning.

Peter, who had just started to hop off to his right, stopped short in sheer astonishment. Just in front of him was a tiny mound of dead leaves, and a few feet beyond Mrs. Teacher was fluttering about on the ground as if badly hurt. Peter simply didn't know what to make of it. Once more he made a movement as if to hop. Teacher flew right down in front of him. "You'll step on my nest!" he cried.

Peter stared, for he didn't see any nest. He said as much.

"It's under that little mound of leaves right in front of your feet!" cried Teacher. "I wasn't going to tell you, but I just had to or you certainly would have stepped on it."

Very carefully Peter walked around the little bunch of leaves and peered under them from the other side. There, sure enough, was a nest beneath them, and in it four speckled eggs. "I won't tell a soul, Teacher. I promise you I won't tell a soul," declared Peter very earnestly. "I understand now why you are called Oven Bird, but I still like the name Teacher best."

Feeling that Mr. and Mrs. Teacher would feel easier in their minds if he left them, Peter said good-by and started on for the lonesome place in the Green Forest where he knew the old nest of Redtail the Hawk had been. As he drew near the place he kept sharp watch through the treetops for a glimpse of Redtail. Presently he saw him high in the blue sky, sailing lazily in big circles. Then Peter became very, very cautious. He tiptoed forward, keeping under cover as much as possible. At last, peeping out from beneath a little hemlock-tree, he could see Redtail's old nest. He saw right away that it was bigger than it had been when he saw it last. Suddenly there was a chorus of hungry cries and Peter saw Mrs. Redtail approaching with a Mouse in her claws. From where he sat he could see four funny heads stretched above the edge of the nest.

"Redtail is using his old nest again and has got a family already," exclaimed Peter. "I guess this is no place for me. The sooner I get away from here the better."

Just then Redtail himself dropped down out of the blue, blue sky and alighted on a tree close at hand. Peter decided that the best thing he could do was to sit perfectly still where he was. He had a splendid view of Redtail, and he couldn't help but admire this big member of the Hawk family. The upper parts of his coat were a dark grayish-brown mixed with touches of chestnut color. The upper part of his breast was streaked with grayish-brown and buff, the lower part having but few streaks. Below this were black spots and bars ending in white. But it was the tail which Peter noticed most of all. It was a rich reddish-brown with a narrow black band near its end and a white tip. Peter understood at once why this big Hawk is called Redtail.

It was not until Mr. and Mrs. Redtail had gone in quest of more food for their hungry youngsters that Peter dared steal away. As soon as he felt it safe to do so, he headed for home as fast as he could go, lipperty-lipperty-lip. He knew that he wouldn't feel safe until that lonesome place in the Green Forest was far behind.

Yet if the truth be known, Peter had less cause to worry than would have been the case had it been some other member of the Hawk family instead of Redtail. And while Redtail and his wife do sometimes catch some of their feathered and furred neighbors, and once in a while a chicken, they do vastly more good than harm.

XIX. A Maker of Thunder and a Friend in Black.

Peter Rabbit's intentions were of the best. Once safely away from that lonesome part of the Green Forest where was the home of Redtail the Hawk, he intended to go straight back to the dear Old Briar-patch. But he was not halfway there when from another direction in the Green Forest there came a sound that caused him to stop short and quite forget all about home. It was a sound very like distant thunder. It began slowly at first and then went faster and faster. Boom—Boom—Boom—Boom-Boom-Boom Boo-Boo-B-B-B-B-b-b-b-b-boom! It was like the long roll on a bass drum.

Peter laughed right out. "That's Strutter the Stuffed Grouse!" he cried joyously. "I had forgotten all about him. I certainly must go over and pay him a call and find out where Mrs. Grouse is. My, how Strutter can drum!"

Peter promptly headed towards that distant thunder. As he drew nearer to it, it sounded louder and louder. Presently Peter stopped to try to locate exactly the place where that sound, which now was more than ever like thunder, was coming from. Suddenly Peter remembered something. "I know just where he is," said he to himself. "There's a big, mossy, hollow log over yonder, and I remember that Mrs. Grouse once told me that that is Strutter's thunder log."

Very, very carefully Peter stole forward, making no sound at all. At last he reached a place where he could peep out and see that big, mossy, hollow log. Sure enough, there was Strutter the Ruffed Grouse. When Peter first saw him he was crouched on one end of the log, a fluffy ball of reddish-brown, black and gray feathers. He was resting. Suddenly he straightened up to

STRUTTER THE RUFFED GROUSE. The black ruff around his neck gives him his name.

his full height, raised his tail and spread it until it was like an open fan above his back. The outer edge was gray, then came a broad band of black, followed by bands of gray, brown and black. Around his neck was a wonderful ruff of black. His reddish-brown wings were dropped until the tips nearly touched the log. His full breast rounded out and was buff color with black markings. He was of about the size of the little Bantam hens Peter had seen in Farmer Brown's henyard.

In the most stately way you can imagine Strutter walked the length of that mossy log. He was a perfect picture of pride as he strutted very much like Tom Gobbler the big Turkey cock. When he reached the end of the log he suddenly dropped his tail, stretched himself to his full height and his wings began to beat, first slowly then faster and faster, until they were just a blur. They seemed to touch above his back but when they came down they didn't quite strike his sides. It was those fast moving wings that made the thunder. It was so loud that Peter almost wanted to stop his ears. When it ended Strutter settled down to rest and once more appeared like a ball of fluffy feathers. His ruff was laid flat.

Peter watched him thunder several times and then ventured to show himself. "Strutter, you are wonderful! simply wonderful!" cried Peter, and he meant just what he said.

Strutter threw out his chest proudly. "That is just what Mrs. Grouse says," he replied. "I don't know of any better thunderer if I do say it myself."

"Speaking of Mrs. Grouse, where is she?" asked Peter eagerly.

"Attending to her household affairs, as a good housewife should," retorted Strutter promptly.

"Do you mean she has a nest and eggs?" asked Peter.

Strutter nodded. "She has twelve eggs," he added proudly.

"I suppose," said Peter artfully, "her nest is somewhere near here on the ground."

"It's on the ground, Peter, but as to where it is I am not saying a word. It may or it may not be near here. Do you want to hear me thunder again?"

Of course Peter said he did, and that was sufficient excuse for Strutter to show off. Peter stayed a while longer to gossip, but finding Strutter more interested in thundering than in talking, he once more started for home.

"I really would like to know where that nest is," said he to himself as he scampered along. "I suppose Mrs. Grouse has hidden it so cleverly that it is quite useless to look for it."

On his way he passed a certain big tree. All around the ground was carpeted with brown, dead leaves. There were no bushes or young trees there. Peter never once thought of looking for a nest. It was the last place in the world he would expect to find one. When he was well past the big tree there was a soft chuckle and from among the brown leaves right at the foot of that big tree a head with a pair of the brightest eyes was raised a little. Those eyes twinkled as they watched Peter out of sight.

"He didn't see me at all," chuckled Mrs. Grouse, as she settled down once more. "That is what comes of having a cloak so like the color of these nice brown leaves. He isn't the first one who has passed me without seeing me at all. It is better than trying to hide a nest, and I certainly am thankful to Old Mother Nature for the cloak she gave me. I wonder if every one of these twelve eggs will hatch. If they do, I certainly will have a family to be proud of."

Meanwhile Peter hurried on in his usual happy-go-lucky fashion until he came to the edge of the Green Forest. Out on the Green Meadows just beyond he caught sight of a black form walking about in a stately way and now and then picking up something. It reminded him of Blacky the Crow, but he knew right away that it wasn't Blacky, because it was so much smaller, being not more than half as big.

"It's Creaker the Grackle. He was one of the first to arrive this spring and I'm ashamed of myself for not having called on him," thought Peter, as he hopped out and started across the Green Meadows towards Creaker. "What a splendid long tail he has. I believe Jenny Wren told me that he belongs to the Blackbird family. He looks so much like Blacky the Crow that I suppose this is why they call him Crow Blackbird."

Just then Creaker turned in such a way that the sun fell full on his head and back. "Why! Why-ee!" exclaimed Peter, rubbing his eyes with astonishment. "He isn't just black! He's beautiful, simply beautiful, and I've always supposed he was just plain, homely black."

It was true. Creaker the Grackle with the sun shining on him was truly beautiful. His head and neck, his throat and upper breast, were a shining blue-black, while his back was a rich, shining brassy-green. His wings and tail were much like his head and neck. As Peter watched it seemed as if the colors were constantly changing. This changing of colors is called iridescence. One other thing Peter noticed and this was that Creaker's eyes were yellow. Just at the moment Peter couldn't remember any other bird with yellow eyes.

"Creaker," cried Peter, "I wonder if you know how handsome you are!"

"I'm glad you think so," replied Creaker. "I'm not at all vain, but there are mighty few birds I would change coats with."

"Is—is—Mrs. Creaker dressed as handsomely as you are?" asked Peter rather timidly.

Creaker shook his head. "Not quite," said he. "She likes plain black better. Some of the feathers on her back shine like mine, but she says that she has no time to show off in the sun and to take care of fine feathers."

"Where is she now?" asked Peter.

"Over home," replied Creaker, pulling a white grub out of the roots of the grass. "We've got a nest over there in one of those pine-trees on the edge of the Green Forest and I expect any day now we will have four hungry babies to feed. I shall have to get busy then. You know I am one of those who believe that every father should do his full share in taking care of his family."

"I'm glad to hear you say it," declared Peter, nodding his head with approval quite as if he was himself the best of fathers, which he isn't at all.

"May I ask you a very personal question, Creaker?"

"Ask as many questions as you like. I don't have to answer them unless I want to," retorted Creaker.

"Is it true that you steal the eggs of other birds?" Peter blurted the question out rather hurriedly.

Creaker's yellow eyes began to twinkle. "That is a very personal question," said he. "I won't go so far as to say I steal eggs, but I've found that eggs are very good for my constitution and if I find a nest with nobody around I sometimes help myself to the eggs. You see the owner might not come back and then those eggs would spoil, and that would be a pity."

"That's no excuse at all," declared Peter. "I believe you're no better than Sammy Jay and Blacky the Crow."

Creaker chuckled, but he did not seem to be at all offended. Just then he heard Mrs. Creaker calling him and with a hasty farewell he spread his wings and headed for the Green Forest. Once in the air he seemed just plain black. Peter watched him out of sight and then once more headed for the dear Old Briar-patch.

XX. A Fisherman Robbed.

Just out of curiosity, and because he possesses what is called the wandering foot, which means that he delights to roam about, Peter Rabbit had run over to the bank of the Big River. There were plenty of bushes, clumps of tall grass, weeds and tangles of vines along the bank of the Big River, so that Peter felt quite safe there. He liked to sit gazing out over the water and wonder where it all came from and where it was going and what, kept it moving.

He was doing this very thing on this particular morning when he happened to glance up in the blue, blue sky. There he saw a broad-winged bird sailing in wide, graceful circles. Instantly Peter crouched a little lower in his hiding-place, for he knew this for a member of the Hawk family and Peter has learned by experience that the only way to keep perfectly safe when one of these hook-clawed, hook-billed birds is about is to keep out of sight.

So now he crouched very close to the ground and kept his eyes fixed on the big bird sailing so gracefully high up in the blue, blue sky over the Big River. Suddenly the stranger paused in his flight and for a moment appeared to remain in one place, his great wings heating rapidly to hold him there. Then those wings were closed and with a rush he shot down straight for the water, disappearing with a great splash. Instantly Peter sat up to his full height that he might see better.

"It's Plunger the Osprey fishing, and I've nothing to fear from him," he cried happily.

Out of the water, his great wings flapping, rose Plunger. Peter looked eagerly to see if he had caught a fish, but there was nothing in Plunger's great, curved claws. Either that fish had been too deep or had seen Plunger and darted away just in the nick of time. Peter had a splendid view of Plunger. He was just a little bigger than Redtail the Hawk. Above he was dark brown, his head and neck marked with white. His tail was grayish, crossed by several narrow dark bands and tipped with white. His under parts were white with some light brown spots on his breast. Peter could see clearly the great, curved claws which are Plunger's fishhooks.

Up, up, up he rose, going round and round in a spiral. When he was well up in the blue, blue sky, he began to sail again in wide circles as when Peter had first seen him. It wasn't long before he again paused and then shot down towards the water. This time he abruptly spread his great wings just before reaching the water so that he no more than wet his feet. Once more a fish had escaped him. But Plunger seemed not in the least discouraged. He is a true fisherman and every true fisherman possesses patience. Up again he spiraled until he was so high that Peter wondered how he could possibly see a fish so far below. You see, Peter didn't know that it is easier to see down into the water from high above it than from close to it. Then, too, there are no more wonderful eyes than those possessed by the members of the Hawk family. And Plunger the Osprey is a Hawk, usually called Fish Hawk.

A third time Plunger shot down and this time, as in his first attempt, he struck the water with a great splash and disappeared. In an instant he reappeared, shaking the water from him in a silver spray and flapping heavily. This time Peter could see a great shining fish in his claws. It was heavy, as Peter could tell by the way in which Plunger flew. He headed towards a tall tree on the other bank of the Big River, there to enjoy his breakfast. He was not more than halfway there when Peter was startled by a harsh scream.

He looked up to see a great bird, with wonderful broad wings, swinging in short circles about Plunger. His body and wings were dark brown, and his head was snowy white, as was his tail. His great hooked beak was yellow and his legs were yellow. Peter knew in an instant who it was. There could be

KING EAGLE, the bald or whiteheaded Eagle. His head, neck and tail are snowy white.

PLUNGER THE OSPREY, one of our largest hawks, brown above and white beneath.

no mistake. It was King Eagle, commonly known as Bald Head, though his head isn't bald at all.

Peter's eyes looked as if they would pop out of his head, for it was quite plain to him that King Eagle was after Plunger, and Peter didn't understand this at all. You see, he didn't understand what King Eagle was screaming. But Plunger did. King Eagle was screaming, "Drop that fish! Drop that fish!"

Plunger didn't intend to drop that fish if he could help himself. It was his fish. Hadn't he caught it himself? He didn't intend to give it up to any robber of the air, even though that robber was King Eagle himself, unless he was actually forced to. So Plunger began to dodge and twist and turn in the air, all the time mounting higher and higher, and all the time screaming harshly, "Robber! Thief! I won't drop this fish! It's mine! It's mine!"

Now the fish was heavy, so of course Plunger couldn't fly as easily and swiftly as if he were carrying nothing. Up, up he went, but all the time King Eagle went up with him, circling round him, screaming harshly, and threatening to strike him with those great cruel, curved claws. Peter watched them, so excited that he fairly danced. "O, I do hope Plunger will get away from that big robber," cried Peter. "He may be king of the air, but he is a robber just the same."

Plunger and King Eagle were now high in the air above the Big River. Suddenly King Eagle swung above Plunger and for an instant seemed to hold himself still there, just as Plunger had done before he had shot down into the water after that fish. There was a still harsher note in King Eagle's scream. If Peter had been near enough he would have seen a look of anger and determination in King Eagle's fierce, yellow eyes. Plunger saw it and knew what it meant. He knew that King Eagle would stand for no more fooling. With a cry of bitter disappointment and anger he let go of the big fish.

Down, down, dropped the fish, shining in the sun like a bar of silver. King Eagle's wings half closed and he shot down like a thunderbolt. Just before the fish reached the water King Eagle struck it with his great claws, checked himself by spreading his broad wings and tail, and then in triumph flew over to the very tree towards which Plunger had started when he had caught the fish. There he leisurely made his breakfast, apparently enjoying it as much as if he had come by it honestly.

As for poor Plunger, he shook himself, screamed angrily once or twice, then appeared to think that it was wisest to make the best of a bad matter and that there were more fish where that one had come from, for he once more began to sail in circles over the Big River, searching for a fish near the surface. Peter watched him until he saw him catch another fish and fly away with it in triumph. King Eagle watched him, too, but having had a good breakfast he was quite willing to let Plunger enjoy his catch in peace.

Late that afternoon Peter visited the Old Orchard, for he just had to tell Jenny Wren all about what he had seen that morning.

"King Eagle is king simply because he is so big and fierce and strong," sputtered Jenny. "He isn't kingly in his habits, not the least bit. He never hesitates to rob those smaller than himself, just as you saw him rob Plunger. He is very fond of fish, and once in a while he catches one for himself when Plunger isn't around to be robbed, but he isn't a very good fisherman, and he isn't the least bit fussy about his fish. Plunger eats only fresh fish which he catches himself, but King Eagle will eat dead fish which he finds on the shore. He doesn't seem to care how long they have been dead either."

"Doesn't he eat anything but fish?" asked Peter innocently.

"Well," retorted Jenny Wren, her eyes twinkling, "I wouldn't advise you to run across the Green Meadows in sight of King Eagle. I am told he is very fond of Rabbit. In fact he is very fond of fresh meat of any kind. He even catches the babies of Lightfoot the Deer when he gets a chance. He is so swift of wing that even the members of the Duck family fear him, for he is especially fond of fat Duck. Even Honker the Goose is not safe from him. King he may be, but he rules only through fear. He is a white-headed old robber. The best thing I can say of him is that he takes a mate for life and is loyal and true to her as long as she lives, and that is a great many years. By the way, Peter, did you know that she is bigger than he is, and that the young during the first year after leaving their nest, are bigger than their parents and do not have white heads? By the time they get white heads they are the same size as their parents."

"That's queer and its hard to believe," said Peter.

"It is queer, but it is true just the same, whether you believe it or not," retorted Jenny Wren, and whisked out of sight into her home.

XXI. A Fishing Party.

Peter Rabbit sat on the edge of the Old Briar-patch trying to make up his mind whether to stay at home, which was the wise and proper thing to do, or to go call on some of the friends he had not yet visited. A sharp, harsh rattle caused him to look up to see a bird about a third larger than Welcome Robin, and with a head out of all proportion to the size of his body. He was flying straight towards the Smiling Pool, rattling harshly as he flew. The mere sound of his voice settled the matter for Peter. "It's Rattles the Kingfisher," he cried. "I think I'll run over to the Smiling Pool and pay him my respects."

So Peter started for the Smiling Pool as fast as his long legs could take him, lipperty-lipperty-lip. He had lost sight of Rattles the Kingfisher, and when he reached the back of the Smiling Pool he was in doubt which way to turn. It was very early in the morning and there was not so much as a ripple on the surface of the Smiling Pool. As Peter sat there trying to make up his mind which way to go, he saw coming from the direction of the Big River a great, broad-winged bird, flying slowly. He seemed to have no neck at all, but carried straight out behind him were two long legs.

"Longlegs the Great Blue Heron! I wonder if he is coming here," exclaimed Peter. "I do hope so."

Peter stayed right where he was and waited. Nearer and nearer came Longlegs. When he was right opposite Peter he suddenly dropped his long legs, folded his great wings, and alighted right on the edge of the Smiling Pool across from where Peter was sitting. If he seemed to have no neck at all when he was flying, now he seemed to be all neck as he stretched it to its full length.

RATTLES THE KINGFISHER. His voice sounds like a watchman's rattle.
TEETER THE SPOTTED SANDPIPER. You can tell him by the way he bobs or teeters.
LONGLEGS THE GREAT BLUE HERON. he stands nearly four feet high.

The fact is, his neck was so long that when he was flying he carried it folded back on his shoulders. Never before had Peter had such an opportunity to see Longlegs.

He stood quite four feet high. The top of his head and throat were white. From the base of his great bill and over his eye was a black stripe which ended in two long, slender, black feathers hanging from the back of his head. His bill was longer than his head, stout and sharp like a spear and yellow in color. His long neck was a light brownish-gray. His back and wings were of a bluish color. The bend of each wing and the feathered parts of his legs were a rusty-red. The remainder of his legs and his feet were black. Hanging down over his breast were beautiful long pearly-gray feathers quite unlike any Peter had seen on any of his other feathered friends. In spite of the length of his legs and the length of his neck he was both graceful and handsome.

"I wonder what has brought him over to the Smiling Pool," thought Peter.

He didn't have to wait long to find out. After standing perfectly still with his neck stretched to its full height until he was sure that no danger was near, Longlegs waded into the water a few steps, folded his neck back on his shoulders until his long bill seemed to rest on his breast, and then remained as motionless as if there were no life in him. Peter also sat perfectly still. By and by he began to wonder if Longlegs had gone to sleep. His own patience was reaching an end and he was just about to go on in search of Rattles the Kingfisher when like a flash the dagger-like bill of Longlegs shot out and down into the water. When he withdrew it Peter saw that Longlegs had caught a little fish which he at once proceeded to swallow head-first. Peter almost laughed right out as he watched the funny efforts of Longlegs to gulp that fish down his long throat. Then Longlegs resumed his old position as motionless as before.

It was no trouble now for Peter to sit still, for he was too interested in watching this lone fisherman to think of leaving. It wasn't long before Longlegs made another catch and this time it was a fat Pollywog. Peter thought of how he had watched Plunger the Osprey fishing in the Big River and the difference in the ways of the two fishermen.

"Plunger hunts for his fish while Longlegs waits for his fish to come to him," thought Peter. "I wonder if Longlegs never goes hunting."

As if in answer to Peter's thought Longlegs seemed to conclude that no more fish were coming his way. He stretched himself up to his full height, looked sharply this way and that way to make sure that all was safe, then began to walk along the edge of the Smiling Pool. He put each foot down slowly and carefully so as to make no noise. He had gone but a few steps when that great bill darted down like a flash, and Peter saw that he had caught a careless young Frog. A few steps farther on he caught another Pollywog. Then coming to a spot that suited him, he once more waded in and began to watch for fish.

Peter was suddenly reminded of Rattles the Kingfisher, whom he had quite forgotten. From the Big Hickory-tree on the bank, Rattles flew out over the Smiling Pool, hovered for an instant, then plunged down head-first. There was a splash, and a second later Rattles was in the air again, shaking the water from him in a silver spray. In his long, stout, black bill was a little fish. He flew back to a branch of the Big Hickory-tree that hung out over the water and thumped the fish against the branch until it was dead. Then he turned it about so he could swallow it head-first. It was a big fish for the size of the fisherman and he had a dreadful time getting it down. But at last it was down, and Rattles set himself to watch for another. The sun shone full on him, and Peter gave a little gasp of surprise.

"I never knew before how handsome Rattles is," thought Peter. He was about the size of Yellow Wing the Flicker, but his head made him look bigger than he really was. You see, the feathers on top of his head stood up in a crest, as if they had been brushed the wrong way. His head, back, wings and tail were a bluish-gray. His throat was white and he wore a white collar. In front of each eye was a little white spot. Across his breast was a belt of bluish-gray, and underneath he was white. There were tiny spots of white on his wings, and his tail was spotted with white. His bill was black and, like that of Longlegs, was long, and stout, and sharp. It looked almost too big for his size.

Presently Rattles flew out and plunged into the Smiling Pool again, this time, very near to where Longlegs was patiently waiting. He caught a fish, for it is not often that Rattles misses. It was smaller than the first one Peter had seen him catch, and this time as soon as he got back to the Big Hickory-tree, he swallowed it without thumping it against the branch. As for Longlegs, he looked thoroughly put out. For a moment or two he stood glaring angrily up at Rattles. You see, when Rattles had plunged so close to Longlegs he had frightened all the fish. Finally Longlegs seemed to make up his mind that there was room for but one fisherman at a time at the Smiling Pool. Spreading his great wings, folding his long neck back on his shoulders, and dragging his long legs out behind him, he flew heavily away in the direction of the Big River.

Rattles remained long enough to catch another little fish, and then with a harsh rattle flew off down the Laughing Brook. "I would know him anywhere by that rattle," thought Peter. "There isn't any one who can make a noise anything like it. I wonder where he has gone to now. He must have a nest, but I haven't the least idea what kind of a nest he builds. Hello! There's Grandfather Frog over on his green lily pad. Perhaps he can tell me."

So Peter hopped along until he was near enough to talk to Grandfather Frog. "What kind of a nest does Rattles the Kingfisher build?" repeated Grandfather Frog. "Chug-arum, Peter Rabbit! I thought everybody knew that Rattles doesn't build a nest. At least I wouldn't call it a nest. He lives in a hole in the ground."

"What!" cried Peter, and looked as if he couldn't believe his own ears.

Grandfather Frog grinned and his goggly eyes twinkled. "Yes," said he, "Rattles lives in a hole in the ground."

"But—but—but what kind of a hole?" stammered Peter.

"Just plain hole," retorted Grandfather Frog, grinning more broadly than ever. Then seeing how perplexed and puzzled Peter looked, he went on to explain. "He usually picks out a high gravelly bank close to the water and digs a hole straight in just a little way from the top. He makes it just big enough for himself and Mrs. Rattles to go in and out of comfortably, and he digs it straight in for several feet. I'm told that at the end of it he makes a sort of bedroom, because he usually has a good-sized family."

"Do you mean to say that he digs it himself?" asked Peter.

Grandfather Frog nodded. "If he doesn't, Mrs. Kingfisher does," he replied. "Those big bills of theirs are picks as well as fish spears. They loosen the sand with those and scoop it out with their feet. I've never seen the inside of their home myself, but I'm told that their bedroom is lined with fish bones. Perhaps you may call that a nest, but I don't."

"I'm going straight down the Laughing Brook to look for that hole," declared Peter, and left in such a hurry that he forgot to be polite enough to say thank you to Grandfather Frog.

XXII. Some Feathered Diggers.

Peter Rabbit scampered along down one bank of the Laughing Brook, eagerly watching for a high, gravelly bank such as Grandfather Frog had said that Rattles the Kingfisher likes to make his home in. If Peter had stopped to do a little thinking, he would have known that he was simply wasting time. You see, the Laughing Brook was flowing through the Green Meadows, so of course there would be no high, gravelly bank, because the Green Meadows are low. But Peter Rabbit, in his usual heedless way, did no thinking. He had seen Rattles fly down the Laughing Brook, and so he had just taken it for granted that the home of Rattles must be somewhere down there.

At last Peter reached the place where the Laughing Brook entered the Big River. Of course he hadn't found the home of Rattles. But now he did find something that for the time being made him quite forget Rattles and his home. Just before it reached the Big River the Laughing Brook wound through a swamp in which were many tall trees and a great number of young trees. A great many big ferns grew there and were splendid to hide under. Peter always did like that swamp.

He had stopped to rest in a clump of ferns when he was startled by seeing a great bird alight in a tree just a little way from him. His first thought was that it was a Hawk, so you can imagine how surprised and pleased he was to discover that it was Mrs. Longlegs. Somehow Peter had always thought of Longlegs the Blue Heron as never alighting anywhere except on the ground. But here was Mrs. Longlegs in a tree. Having nothing to fear, Peter crept out from his hiding place that he might see better.

In the tree in which Mrs. Longlegs was perched and just below her he saw a little platform of sticks. He didn't suspect that it was a nest, because it looked too rough and loosely put together to be a nest. Probably he wouldn't have thought about it at all had not Mrs. Longlegs settled herself on it right while Peter was watching. It didn't seem big enough or strong enough to hold her, but it did.

"As I live," thought Peter, "I've found the nest of Longlegs! He and Mrs. Longlegs may be good fishermen but they certainly are mighty poor nest-builders. I don't see how under the sun Mrs. Longlegs ever gets on and off that nest without kicking the eggs out."

Peter sat around for a while, but as he didn't care to let his presence be known, and as there was no one to talk to, he presently made up his mind that being so near the Big River he would go over there to see if Plunger the Osprey was fishing again on this day.

When he reached the Big River, Plunger was not in sight. Peter was disappointed. He had just about made up his mind to return the way he had come, when from beyond the swamp, farther up the Big River, he heard the harsh, rattling cry of Rattles the Kingfisher. It reminded him of what he had come for, and he at once began to hurry in that direction.

Peter came out of the swamp on a little sandy beach. There he squatted for a moment, blinking his eyes, for out there the sun was very bright. Then a little way beyond him he discovered something that in his eager curiosity made him quite forget that he was out in the open where it was anything but safe for a Rabbit to be. What he saw was a high sandy bank. With a hasty glance this way and that way to make sure that no enemy was in sight, Peter scampered along the edge of the water till he was right at the foot of that sandy bank. Then he squatted down and looked eagerly for a hole such as he imagined Rattles the Kingfisher might make. Instead of one hole he saw a lot of holes, but they were very small holes. He knew right away that Rattles couldn't possibly get in or out of a single one of those holes. In fact, those holes in the bank were no bigger than the holes Downy the Woodpecker makes in trees. Peter couldn't imagine who or what had made them.

As Peter sat there staring and wondering a trim little head appeared at the entrance to one of those holes. It was a trim little head with a very small bill and a snowy white throat. At first glance Peter thought it was his old friend, Skimmer the Tree Swallow, and he was just on the point of asking what under the sun Skimmer was doing in such a place as that, when with a lively twitter of greeting the owner of that little hole in the bank flew out and circled over Peter's head. It wasn't Skimmer at all. It was Banker the Bank Swallow, own cousin to Skimmer the Tree Swallow. Peter recognized him the instant he got a full view of him.

In the first place Banker was a little smaller than Skimmer. Then too, he was not nearly so handsome. His back, instead of being that beautiful rich steel-blue which makes Skimmer so handsome, was a sober grayish-brown. He was a little darker on his wings and tail. His breast, instead of being all snowy white, was crossed with a brownish band. His tail was more nearly square across the end than is the case with other members of the Swallow family.

"Wha—wha—what were you doing there?" stuttered Peter, his eyes popping right out with curiosity and excitement.

"Why, that's my home," twittered Banker.

"Do—do—do you mean to say that you live in a hole in the ground?" cried Peter.

"Certainly; why not?" twittered Banker as he snapped up a fly just over Peter's head.

"I don't know any reason why you shouldn't," confessed Peter. "But somehow it is hard for me to think of birds as living in holes in the ground. I've only just found out that Rattles the Kingfisher does. But I didn't suppose there were any others. Did you make that hole yourself, Banker?"

"Of course," replied Banker. "That is, I helped make it. Mrs. Banker did her share. 'Way in at the end of it we've got the nicest little nest of straw and feathers. What is more, we've got four white eggs in there, and Mrs. Banker is sitting on them now."

By this time the air seemed to be full of Banker's friends, skimming and circling this way and that, and going in and out of the little holes in the bank.

"I am like my big cousin, Twitter the Purple Martin, fond of society," explained Banker. "We Bank Swallows like our homes close together. You said that you had just learned that Rattles the Kingfisher has his home in a bank. Do you know where it is?"

"No," replied Peter. "I was looking for it when I discovered your home. Can you tell me where it is?"

"I'll do better than that;" replied Banker. "I'll show you where it is."

He darted some distance up along the bank and hovered for an instant close to the top. Peter scampered over there and looked up. There, just a few inches below the top, was another hole, a very much larger hole than those he had just left. As he was staring up at it a head with a long sharp bill and a crest which looked as if all the feathers on the top of his head had been brushed the wrong way, was thrust out. It was Rattles himself. He didn't seem at all glad to see Peter. In fact, he came out and darted at Peter angrily. Peter didn't wait to feel that sharp dagger-like bill. He took to his heels. He had seen what he started out to find and he was quite content to go home.

Peter took a short cut across the Green Meadows. It took him past a certain tall, dead tree. A sharp cry of "Kill-ee, kill-ee, kill-ee!" caused Peter to look up just in time to see a trim, handsome bird whose body was about the size of Sammy Jay's but whose longer wings and longer tail made him look bigger. One glance was enough to tell Peter that this was a member of the Hawk family, the smallest of the family. It was Killy the Sparrow Hawk. He is too small for Peter to fear him, so now Peter was possessed of nothing more than a very lively curiosity, and sat up to watch.

Out over the meadow grass Killy sailed. Suddenly, with beating wings, he kept himself in one place in the air and then dropped down into the grass. He was up again in an instant, and Peter could see that he had a fat grasshopper in his claws. Back to the top of the tall, dead tree he flew and there ate the grasshopper. When it was finished he sat up straight and still, so still that he seemed a part of the tree itself. With those wonderful eyes of his he was watching for another grasshopper or for a careless Meadow Mouse.

Very trim and handsome was Killy. His back was reddish-brown crossed by bars of black. His tail was reddish-brown with a band of black near its end and a white tip. His wings were slaty-blue with little bars of black, the longest feathers leaving white bars. Underneath he was a beautiful buff, spotted with black. His head was bluish with a reddish patch right on top. Before and behind each ear was a black mark. His rather short bill, like the bills of all the rest of his family, was hooked.

As Peter sat there admiring Killy, for he was handsome enough for any one to admire, he noticed for the first time a hole high up in the trunk of the tree, such a hole as Yellow Wing the Flicker might have made and probably did make. Right away Peter remembered what Jenny Wren had told him about Killy's making his nest in just such a hole. "I wonder," thought Peter, "if that is Killy's home."

Just then Killy flew over and dropped in the grass just in front of Peter, where he caught another fat grasshopper. "Is that your home up there?" asked Peter hastily.

"It certainly is, Peter," replied Killy. "This is the third summer Mrs. Killy and I have had our home there."

"You seem to be very fond of grasshoppers," Peter ventured.

"I am," replied Killy. "They are very fine eating when one can get enough of them."

"Are they the only kind of food you eat?" ventured Peter.

Killy laughed. It was a shrill laugh. "I should say not," said he. "I eat spiders and worms and all sorts of insects big enough to give a fellow a decent bite. But for real good eating give me a fat Meadow Mouse. I don't object to a Sparrow or some other small bird now and then, especially when I have a family of hungry youngsters to feed. But take it the season through, I live mostly on grasshoppers and insects and Meadow Mice. I do a lot of good in this world, I'd have you know."

Peter said that he supposed that this was so, but all the time he kept thinking what a pity it was that Killy ever killed his feathered neighbors. As soon as he conveniently could he politely bade Killy good-by and hurried home to the dear Old Briar-patch, there to think over how queer it seemed that a member of the hawk family should nest in a hollow tree and a member of the Swallow family should dig a hole in the ground.

XXIII. SOME BIG MOUTHS.

BOOM! PETER Rabbit jumped as if he had been shot. It was all so sudden and unexpected that Peter jumped before he had time to think. Then he looked foolish. He felt foolish. He had been scared when there was nothing to be afraid of.

"Ha, ha, ha, ha," tittered Jenny Wren. "What are you jumping for, Peter Rabbit? That was only Boomer the Nighthawk."

"I know it just as well as you do, Jenny Wren," retorted Peter rather crossly. "You know being suddenly startled is apt to make people feel cross. If I had seen him anywhere about he wouldn't have made me jump. It was the unexpectedness of it. I don't see what he is out now for, anyway, It isn't even dusk yet, and I thought him a night bird."

"So he is," retorted Jenny Wren. "Anyway, he is a bird of the evening, and that amounts to the same thing. But just because he likes the evening best isn't any reason why he shouldn't come out in the daylight, is it?"

"No-o," replied Peter rather slowly. "I don't suppose it is."

"Of course it isn't," declared Jenny Wren. "I see Boomer late in the afternoon nearly every day. On cloudy days I often see him early in the afternoon. He's a queer fellow, is Boomer. Such a mouth as he has! I suppose it is very handy to have a big mouth if one must catch all one's food in the air, but it certainly isn't pretty when it is wide open."

"I never saw a mouth yet that was pretty when it was wide open," retorted Peter, who was still feeling a little put out. "I've never noticed that Boomer has a particularly big mouth."

"Well he has, whether you've noticed it or not," retorted Jenny Wren sharply. "He's got a little bit of a bill, but a great big mouth. I don't see what folks call him a Hawk for when he isn't a Hawk at all. He is no more of a Hawk than I am, and goodness knows I'm not even related to the Hawk family."

"I believe you told me the other day that Boomer is related to Sooty the Chimney Swift," said Peter.

Jenny nodded vigorously. "So I did, Peter," she replied. "I'm glad you have such a good memory. Boomer and Sooty are sort of second cousins. There is Boomer now, way up in the sky. I do wish he'd dive and scare some one else."

Peter tipped his head 'way back. High up in the blue, blue sky was a bird which at that distance looked something like a much overgrown Swallow. He was circling and darting about this way and that. Even while Peter watched he half closed his wings and shot down with such speed that Peter actually held his breath. It looked very, very much as if Boomer would dash himself to pieces. Just before he reached the earth he suddenly opened those wings and turned upward. At the instant he turned, the booming sound which had so startled Peter was heard. It was made by the rushing of the wind through the larger feathers of his wings as he checked himself.

In this dive Boomer had come near enough for Peter to get a good look at him. His coat seemed to be a mixture of brown and gray, very soft looking. His wings were brown with a patch of white on each. There was a white patch on his throat and a band of white near the end of his tail.

"He's rather handsome, don't you think?" asked Jenny Wren.

"He certainly is," replied Peter. "Do you happen to know what kind of a nest the Nighthawks build, Jenny?"

"They don't build any." Jenny Wren was a picture of scorn as she said this. "They don't built any nests at all. It can't be because they are lazy for I don't know of any birds that hunt harder for their living than do Boomer and Mrs. Boomer."

"But if there isn't any nest where does Mrs. Boomer lay her eggs?" cried Peter. "I think you must be mistaken, Jenny Wren. They must have some kind of a nest. Of course they must."

"Didn't I say they don't have a nest?" sputtered Jenny. "Mrs. Nighthawk doesn't lay but two eggs, anyway. Perhaps she thinks it isn't worth while building a nest for just two eggs. Anyway, she lays them on the ground or on a flat rock and lets it go at that. She isn't quite as bad as Sally Sly the Cowbird, for she does sit on those eggs and she is a good mother. But just think of those Nighthawk children never having any home! It doesn't seem to me right and it never will. Did you ever see Boomer in a tree?"

Peter shook his head. "I've seen him on the ground," said he, "but I never have seen him in a tree. Why did you ask, Jenny Wren?"

"To find out how well you have used your eyes," snapped Jenny. "I just wanted to see if you had noticed anything peculiar about the way he sits in a tree. But as long as you haven't seen him in a tree I may as well tell you that he doesn't sit as most birds do. He sits lengthwise of a branch. He never sits across it as the rest of us do."

"How funny!" exclaimed Peter. "I suppose that is Boomer making that queer noise we hear."

"Yes," replied Jenny. "He certainly does like to use his voice. They tell me that some folks call him Bullbat, though why they should call him either Bat or Hawk is beyond me. I suppose you know his cousin, Whip-poor-will."

"I should say I do," replied Peter. "He's enough to drive one crazy when he begins to shout 'Whip poor Will' close at hand. That voice of his goes through me so that I want to stop both ears. There isn't a person of my acquaintance who can say a thing over and over, over and over, so many times without stopping for breath. Do I understand that he is cousin to Boomer?"

"He is a sort of second cousin, the same as Sooty the Chimney Swift," explained Jenny Wren. "They look enough alike to be own cousins. Whip-poor-will has just the same kind of a big mouth and he is dressed very much like Boomer, save that there are no white patches on his wings."

"I've noticed that," said Peter. "That is one way I can tell them apart."

"So you noticed that much, did you?" cried Jenny. "It does you credit, Peter. It does you credit. I wonder if you also noticed Whip-poor-will's whiskers."

"Whiskers!" cried Peter. "Who ever heard of a bird having whiskers? You can stuff a lot down me, Jenny Wren, but there are some things I cannot swallow, and bird whiskers is one of them."

"Nobody asked you to swallow them. Nobody wants you to swallow them," snapped Jenny. "I don't know why a bird shouldn't have whiskers just as well as you, Peter Rabbit. Anyway, Whip-poor-will has them and that is all there is to it. It doesn't make any difference whether you believe in them or not, they are there. And I guess Whip-poor-will finds them just as useful as you find yours, and a little more so. I know this much, that if I had to catch all my food in the air I'd want whiskers and lots of them so that the insects would get tangled in them. I suppose that's what Whip-poor-will's are for."

"I beg your pardon, Jenny Wren," said Peter very humbly. "Of course Whip-poor-will has whiskers if you say so. By the way, do the Whip-poor-wills do any better in the matter of a nest than the Nighthawks?"

"Not a bit," replied Jenny Wren. "Mrs. Whip-poor-will lays her eggs right on the ground, but usually in the Green Forest where it is dark and lonesome. Like Mrs. Nighthawk, she lays only two. It's the same way with another second cousin, Chuck-will's-widow."

"Who?" cried Peter, wrinkling his brows.

"Chuck-will's-widow," Jenny Wren fairly shouted it. "Don't you know Chuck-will's-widow?"

Peter shook his head. "I never heard of such a bird," he confessed.

"That's what comes of never having traveled," retorted Jenny Wren. "If you'd ever been in the South the way I have you would know Chuck-will's-widow. He looks a whole lot like the other two we've been talking about, but has even a bigger mouth. What's more, he has whiskers with branches. Now you needn't look as if you doubted that, Peter Rabbit; it's so. In his habits he's just like his cousins, no nest and only two eggs. I never saw people so afraid to raise a real family. If the Wrens didn't do better than that, I don't know what would become of us." You know Jenny usually has a family of six or eight.

XXIV. The Warblers Arrive.

If there is one family of feathered friends which perplexes Peter Rabbit more than another, it is the Warbler family.

"So many of them come together and they move about so constantly that a fellow doesn't have a chance to look at one long enough to recognize him," complained Peter to Jenny Wren one morning when the Old Orchard was fairly alive with little birds no bigger than Jenny Wren herself.

And such restless little folks as they were!

They were not still an instant, flitting from tree to tree, twig to twig, darting out into the air and all the time keeping up an endless chattering mingled with little snatches of song. Peter would no sooner fix his eyes on one than another entirely different in appearance would take its place. Occasionally he would see one whom he recognized, one who would stay for the nesting season. But the majority of them would stop only for a day or two, being bound farther north to make their summer homes.

Apparently, Jenny Wren did not look upon them altogether with favor. Perhaps Jenny was a little bit envious, for compared with the bright colors of some of them Jenny was a very homely small person indeed. Then, too, there were so many of them and they were so busy catching all kinds of small insects that it may be Jenny was a little fearful they would not leave enough for her to get her own meals easily.

"I don't see what they have to stop here for," scolded Jenny. "They could just as well go somewhere else where they would not be taking the food out of the mouths of honest folk who are here to stay all summer. Did you ever in your life see such uneasy people? They don't keep still an instant. It positively

SUNSHINE THE YELLOW WARBLER, the one bird who is all yellow.
ZEE-ZEE THE REDSTART, dressed chiefly in black and orange.

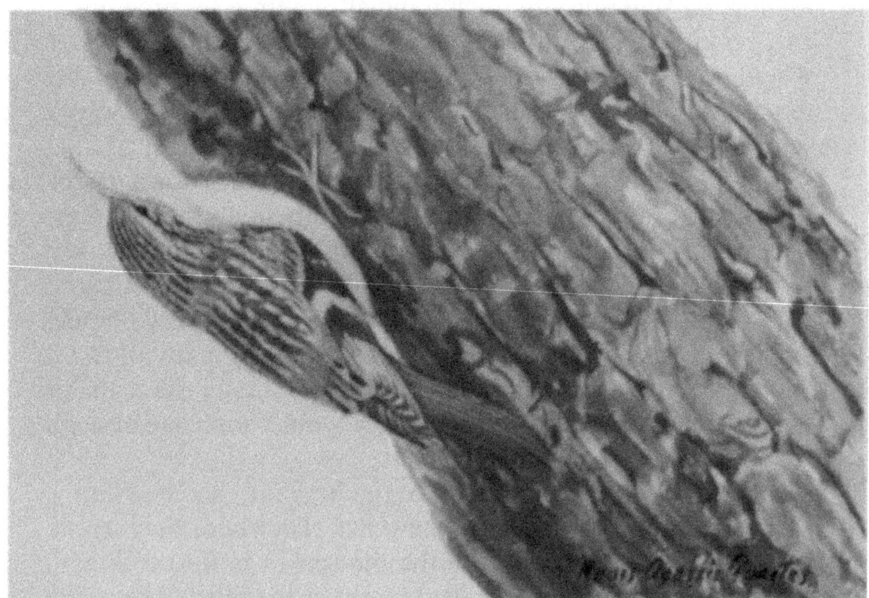

SEEP-SEEP THE BROWN CREEPER. When in winter you see a little brown-backed bird going round and round up a tree trunk it is the Brown Creeper.

makes me tired just to watch them."

Peter couldn't help but chuckle, for Jenny Wren herself is a very restless and uneasy person. As for Peter, he was thoroughly enjoying this visit of the Warblers, despite the fact that he was having no end of trouble trying to tell who was who. Suddenly one darted down and snapped up a fly almost under Peter's very nose and was back up in a tree before Peter could get his breath. "It's Zee Zee the Redstart!" cried Peter joyously. "I would know Zee Zee anywhere. Do you know who he reminds me of, Jenny Wren?"

"Who?" demanded Jenny.

"Goldy the Oriole," replied Peter promptly. "Only of course he's ever and ever so much smaller. He's all black and orange-red and white something as Goldy is, only there isn't quite so much orange on him."

For just an instant Zee Zee sat still with his tail spread. His head, throat and back were black and there was a black band across the end of his tail and a black stripe down the middle of it. The rest was bright orange-red. On each wing was a band of orange-red and his sides were the same color. Underneath he was white tinged more or less with orange.

It was only for an instant that Zee Zee sat still; then he was in the air, darting, diving, whirling, going through all sorts of antics as he caught tiny insects too small for Peter to see. Peter began to wonder how he kept still long enough to sleep at night. And his voice was quite as busy as his wings. "Zee, zee, zee, zee!" he would cry. But this was only one of many notes. At times he would sing a beautiful little song and then again it would seem as if he were trying to imitate other members of the Warbler family.

"I do hope Zee Zee is going to stay here," said Peter. "I just love to watch him."

"He'll stay fast enough," retorted Jenny Wren. "I don't imagine he'll stay in the Old Orchard and I hope he won't, because if he does it will make it just that much harder for me to catch enough to feed my big family. Probably he and Mrs. Redstart will make their home on the edge of the Green Forest. They like it better over there, for which I am thankful. There's Mrs Redstart now. Just notice that where Zee Zee is bright orange-y red she is yellow, and instead of a black head she has a gray head and her back is olive-green with a grayish tinge. She isn't nearly as handsome as Zee Zee, but then, that's not to be expected. She lets Zee Zee do the singing and the showing off and she does the work. I expect she'll build that nest with almost no help at all from him. But Zee Zee is a good father, I'll say that much for him. He'll do his share in feeding their babies."

Just then Peter caught sight of a bird all in yellow. He was about the same size as Zee Zee and was flitting about among the bushes along the old stone wall. "There's Sunshine!" cried Peter, and without being polite enough to even bid Jenny Wren farewell, he scampered over to where he could see the one he called Sunshine flitting about from bush to bush.

"Oh, Sunshine!" he cried, as he came within speaking distance, "I'm ever and ever so glad to see you back. I do hope you and Mrs. Sunshine are going to make your home somewhere near here where I can see you every day."

"Hello, Peter! I am just as glad to see you as you are to see me," cried Sunshine the Yellow Warbler. "Yes, indeed, we certainly intend to stay here if we can find just the right place for our nest. It is lovely to be back here again. We've journeyed so far that we don't want to go a bit farther if we can help it. Have you seen Sally Sly the Cowbird around here this spring?"

Peter nodded. "Yes," said he, "I have."

"I'm sorry to hear it," declared Sunshine. "She made us a lot of trouble last year. But we fooled her."

"How did you fool her?" asked Peter.

Sunshine paused to pick a tiny worm from a leaf. "Well," said he, "she found our nest just after we had finished it and before Mrs. Sunshine had had a chance to lay an egg. Of course you know what she did."

"I can guess," replied Peter. "She laid one of her own eggs in your nest."

Sunshine stopped to pick two or three more worms from the leaves. "Yes," said he. "She did just that, the lazy good-for-nothing creature! But it didn't do her a bit of good, not a bit. That egg never hatched. We fooled her and that's what we'll do again if she repeats that trick this year."

"What did you do, throw that egg out?" asked Peter.

"No," replied Sunshine. "Our nest was too deep for us to get that egg out. We just made a second bottom in our nest right over that egg and built the sides of the nest a little higher. Then we took good care that she didn't have a chance to lay another egg in there."

"Then you had a regular two-story nest, didn't you?" cried Peter, opening his eyes very wide.

Sunshine nodded. "Yes, sir," said he, "and it was a mighty fine nest, if I do say it. If there's anything Mrs. Sunshine and I pride ourselves on it is our nest. There are no babies who have a softer, cozier home than ours."

"What do you make your nest of?" asked Peter.

"Fine grasses and soft fibers from plants, some hair when we can find it, and a few feathers. But we always use a lot of that nice soft fern-cotton. There is nothing softer or nicer that I know of."

All the time Peter had been admiring Sunshine and thinking how wonderfully well he was named. At first glance he seemed to be all yellow, as if somehow he had managed to catch and hold the sunshine in his feathers. There wasn't a white feather on him. When he came very close Peter could see that on his breast and underneath were little streaks of reddish brown and his wings and tail were a little blackish. Otherwise he was all yellow.

Presently he was joined by Mrs. Sunshine. She was not such a bright yellow as was Sunshine, having an olive-green tint on her back. But underneath she was almost clear yellow without the reddish-brown streaks. She too was glad to see Peter but couldn't stop to gossip, for already, as she informed Sunshine, she had found just the place for their nest. Of course Peter begged to be told where it was. But the two little folks in yellow snapped their bright eyes at him and told him that that was their secret and they didn't propose to tell a living soul.

Perhaps if Peter had not been so curious and eager to get acquainted with other members of the Warbler family he would have stayed and done a little spying. As it was, he promised himself to come back to look for that nest after it had been built; then he scurried back among the trees of the Old Orchard to look for other friends among the busy little Warblers who were making the Old Orchard such a lively place that morning.

"There's one thing about it," cried Peter. "Any one can tell Zee Zee the Redstart by his black and flame colored suit. There is no other like it. And any one can tell Sunshine the Yellow Warbler because there isn't anybody else who seems to be all yellow. My, what a lively, lovely lot these Warblers are!"

xxv. Three Cousins Quite Unlike.

As Peter Rabbit passed one of the apple-trees in the Old Orchard, a thin, wiry voice hailed him. "It's a wonder you wouldn't at least say you're glad to see me back, Peter Rabbit," said the voice.

Peter, who had been hopping along rather fast, stopped abruptly to look up. Running along a limb just over his head, now on top and now underneath, was a little bird with a black and white striped coat and a white waistcoat. Just as Peter looked it flew down to near the base of the tree and began to run straight up the trunk, picking things from the bark here and there as it ran. Its way of going up that tree trunk reminded Peter of one of his winter friends, Seep Seep the Brown Creeper.

"It strikes me that this is a mighty poor welcome for one who has just come all the way from South America," said the little black and white bird with twinkling eyes.

"Oh, Creeper, I didn't know you were here!" cried Peter. "You know I'm glad to see you. I'm just as glad as glad can be. You are such a quiet fellow I'm afraid I shouldn't have seen you at all if you hadn't spoken. You know it's always been hard work for me to believe that you are really and truly a Warbler."

"Why so?" demanded Creeper the Black and White Warbler, for that is the name by which he is commonly known. "Why so? Don't I look like a Warbler?"

"Ye-es," said Peter slowly. "You do look like one but you don't act like one."

"In what way don't I act like one I should like to know?" demanded Creeper.

"Well," replied Peter, "all the rest of the Warblers are the uneasiest folks I know of. They can't seem to keep still a minute. They are everlastingly flitting about this way and that way and the other way. I actually get tired watching them. But you are not a bit that way. Then the way you run up tree trunks and along the limbs isn't a bit Warbler-like. Why don't you flit and dart about as the others do?"

Creeper's bright eyes sparkled.

"I don't have to," said he. "I'm going to let you into a little secret, Peter. The rest of them get their living from the leaves and twigs and in the air, but I've discovered an easier way. I've found out that there are lots of little worms and insects and eggs on the trunks and big limbs of the trees and that I can get the best kind of a living there without flitting about everlastingly. I don't have to share them with anybody but the Woodpeckers, Nuthatches, and Tommy Tit the Chickadee."

"That reminds me," said Peter. "Those folks you have mentioned nest in holes in trees; do you?"

"I should say not," retorted Creeper. "I don't know of any Warbler who does. I build on the ground, if you want to know. I nest in the Green Forest. Sometimes I make my nest in a little hollow at the base of a tree; sometimes I put it under a stump or rock or tuck it in under the roots of a tree that has been blown over. But there, Peter Rabbit, I've talked enough. I'm glad you're glad that I'm back, and I'm glad I'm back too."

Creeper continued on up the trunk of the tree, picking here and picking there. Just then Peter caught sight of another friend whom he could always tell by the black mask he wore. It was Mummer the Yellow-throat. He had just darted into the thicket of bushes along the old stone wall. Peter promptly hurried over there to look for him.

When Peter reached the place where he had caught a glimpse of Mummer, no one was to be seen. Peter sat down, uncertain which way to go. Suddenly Mummer popped out right in front of Peter, seemingly from nowhere at all. His throat and breast were bright yellow and his back wings and tail a soft olive-green. But the most remarkable thing about him was the mask of black right across his cheeks, eyes and forehead. At least it looked like a mask, although it really wasn't one.

"Hello, Mummer!" cried Peter.

"Hello yourself, Peter Rabbit!" retorted Mummer and then disappeared as suddenly as he had appeared.

Peter blinked and looked in vain all about.

"Looking for some one?" asked Mummer, suddenly popping into view where Peter least expected him.

"For goodness' sake, can't you sit still a minute?" cried Peter. "How do you expect a fellow can talk to you when he can't keep his eyes on you more than two seconds at a time."

"Who asked you to talk to me?" responded Mummer, and popped out of sight. Two seconds later he was back again and his bright little eyes fairly shone with mischief. Then before Peter could say a word Mummer burst into a pleasant little song. He was so full of happiness that Peter couldn't be cross with him.

"There's one thing I like about you, Mummer," declared Peter, "and that is that I never get you mixed up with anybody else. I should know you just as far as I could see you because of that black mask across your face. Has Mrs. Yellow-throat arrived yet?"

"Certainly," replied another voice, and Mrs. Yellow-throat flitted across right in front of Peter. For just a second she sat still, long enough for him to have one good look at her. She was dressed very like Mummer save that she did not wear the black mask.

Peter was just about to say something polite and pleasant when from just back of him there sounded a loud, very emphatic, "Chut! Chut!" Peter whirled about to find another old friend. It was Chut-Chut the Yellow-breasted Chat, the largest of the Warbler family. He was so much bigger than Mummer that it was hard to believe that they were own cousins. But Peter knew they were, and he also knew that he could never mistake Chut-Chut for any other member of the family because of his big size, which was that of some of the members of the Sparrow family. His back was a dark olive-green, but his throat and breast were a beautiful bright yellow. There was a broad white line above each eye and a little white line underneath. Below his breast he was all white.

To have seen him you would have thought that he suspected Peter might do him some harm. He acted that way. If Peter hadn't known him so well he might have been offended. But Peter knew that there is no one among his feathered friends more cautious than Chut-Chut the Chat. He never takes anything for granted. He appears to be always on the watch for danger, even to the extent of suspecting his very best friends.

When he had decided in his own mind that there was no danger, Chut-Chut came out for a little gossip. But like all the rest of the Warblers he couldn't keep still. Right in the middle of the story of his travels from far-away Mexico he flew to the top of a little tree, began to sing, then flew out into the air with his legs dangling and his tail wagging up and down in the funniest way, and there continued his song as he slowly dropped down into the thicket again. It was a beautiful song and Peter hastened to tell him so.

Chut-Chut was pleased. He showed it by giving a little concert all by himself. It seemed to Peter that he never had heard such a variety of whistles and calls and songs as came from that yellow throat. When it was over Chut-Chut abruptly said good-by and disappeared. Peter could hear his sharp "Chut! Chut!" farther along in the thicket as he hunted for worms among the bushes.

"I wonder," said Peter, speaking out loud without thinking, "where he builds his nest. I wonder if he builds it on the ground, the way Creeper does."

"No," declared Mummer, who all the time had been darting about close at hand. "He doesn't, but I do. Chut-Chut puts his nest near the ground, however, usually within two or three feet. He builds it in bushes or briars. Sometimes if I can find a good tangle of briars I build my nest in it several feet from the ground, but as a rule I would rather have it on the ground under a bush or in a clump of weeds. Have you seen my cousin Sprite the Parula Warbler, yet?"

"Not yet," said Peter, as he started for home.

XXVI. Peter Gets a Lame Neck.

For several days it seemed to Peter Rabbit that everywhere he went he found members of the Warbler family. Being anxious to know all of them he did his best to remember how each one looked, but there were so many and some of them were dressed so nearly alike that after awhile Peter became so mixed that he gave it up as a bad job. Then, as suddenly as they had appeared, the Warblers disappeared. That is to say, most of them disappeared. You see they had only stopped for a visit, being on their way farther north.

In his interest in the affairs of others of his feathered friends, Peter had quite forgotten the Warblers. Then one day when he was in the Green Forest where the spruce-trees grow, he stopped to rest. This particular part of the Green Forest was low and damp, and on many of the trees gray moss grew, hanging down from the branches and making the trees look much older than they really were. Peter was staring at a hanging branch of this moss without thinking anything about it when suddenly a little bird alighted on it and disappeared in it. At least, that is what Peter thought. But it was all so unexpected that he couldn't be sure his eyes hadn't fooled him.

Of course, right away he became very much interested in that bunch of moss. He stared at it very hard. At first it looked no different from a dozen other bunches of moss, but presently he noticed that it was a little thicker than other bunches, as if somehow it had been woven together. He hopped off to one side so he could see better. It looked as if in one side of that bunch of moss was a little round hole. Peter blinked and looked very hard indeed to make sure. A minute later there was no doubt at all, for a little feathered head was poked out and a second later a dainty mite of a bird flew out and alighted very close to Peter. It was one of the smaller members of the Warbler family.

"Sprite!" cried Peter joyously. "I missed you when your cousins passed through here, and I thought you had gone to the Far North with the rest of them."

"Well, I haven't, and what's more I'm not going to go on to the Far North. I'm going to stay right here," declared Sprite the Parula Warbler, for that is who it was.

As Peter looked at Sprite he couldn't help thinking that there wasn't a daintier member in the whole Warbler family. His coat was of a soft bluish color with a yellowish patch in the very center of his back. Across each wing were two bars of white. His throat was yellow. Just beneath it was a little band of bluish-black. His breast was yellow and his sides were grayish and brownish-chestnut.

"Sprite, you're just beautiful," declared Peter in frank admiration. "What was the reason I didn't see you up in the Old Orchard with your cousins?"

"Because I wasn't there," was Sprite's prompt reply as he flitted about, quite unable to sit still a minute. "I wasn't there because I like the Green Forest better, so I came straight here."

"What were you doing just now in that bunch of moss?" demanded Peter, a sudden suspicion of the truth hopping into his head.

"Just looking it over," replied Sprite, trying to look innocent.

At that very instant Peter looked up just in time to see a tail disappearing in the little round hole in the side of the bunch of moss. He knew that that tail belonged to Mrs. Sprite, and just that glimpse told him all he wanted to know.

"You've got a nest in there!" Peter exclaimed excitedly. "There's no use denying it, Sprite; you've got a nest in there! What a perfectly lovely place for a nest."

Sprite saw at once that it would be quite useless to try to deceive Peter. "Yes," said he, "Mrs. Sprite and I have a nest in there. We've just finished it. I think myself it is rather nice. We always build in moss like this. All we have to do is to find a nice thick bunch and then weave it together at the bottom and line the inside with fine grasses. It looks so much like all the rest of the bunches of moss that it is seldom any one finds it. I wouldn't trade nests with anybody I know."

"Isn't it rather lonesome over here by yourselves?" asked Peter.

"Not at all," replied Sprite. "You see, we are not as much alone as you think. My cousin, Fidget the Myrtle Warbler, is nesting not very far away, and another cousin Weechi the Magnolia Warbler is also quite near. Both have begun housekeeping already."

Of course Peter was all excitement and interest at once. "Where are their homes?" he asked eagerly. "Tell me where they are and I'll go straight over and call."

"Peter," said Sprite severely, "you ought to know better than to ask me to tell you anything of this kind. You have been around enough to know that there is no secret so precious as the secret of a home. You happened to find mine, and I guess I can trust you not to tell anybody where it is. If you can find the homes of Fidget and Weechi, all right, but I certainly don't intend to tell you where they are."

Peter knew that Sprite was quite right in refusing to tell the secrets of his cousins, but he couldn't think of going home without at least looking for those homes. He tried to look very innocent as he asked if they also were in hanging bunches of moss. But Sprite was too smart to be fooled and Peter learned nothing at all.

For some time Peter hopped around this way and that way, thinking every bunch of moss he saw must surely contain a nest. But though he looked and looked and looked, not another little round hole did he find, and there were so many bunches of moss that finally his neck ached from tipping his head back so much. Now Peter hasn't much patience as he might have, so after a while he gave up the search and started on his way home. On higher ground, just above the low swampy place where grew the moss-covered trees, he came to a lot of young hemlock-trees. These had no moss on them. Having given up his search Peter was thinking of other things when there flitted across in front of him a black and gray bird with a yellow cap, yellow sides, and a yellow patch at the root of his tail. Those yellow patches were all Peter needed to see to recognize Fidget the Myrtle Warbler, one of the two friends he had been so long looking for down among the moss-covered trees.

"Oh, Fidget!" cried Peter, hurrying after the restless little bird. "Oh, Fidget! I've been looking everywhere for you."

"Well, here I am," retorted Fidget. "You didn't look everywhere or you would have found me before. What can I do for you?" All the time Fidget was hopping and flitting about, never still an instant.

"You can tell me where your nest is," replied Peter promptly.

"I can, but I won't," retorted Fidget. "Now honestly, Peter, do you think you have any business to ask such a question?"

Peter hung his head and then replied quite honestly, "No I don't, Fidget. But you see Sprite told me that you had a nest not very far from his and I've looked at bunches of moss until I've got a crick in the back of my neck."

"Bunches of moss!" exclaimed Fidget. "What under the sun do you think I have to do with bunches of moss?"

"Why—why—I just thought you probably had your nest in one, the same as your cousin Sprite."

Fidget laughed right out. "I'm afraid you would have a worse crick in the back of your neck than you've got now before ever you found my nest in a bunch of moss," said he. "Moss may suit my cousin Sprite, but it doesn't suit me at all. Besides, I don't like those dark places where the moss grows on the trees. I build my nest of twigs and grass and weed-stalks and I line it with hair and rootlets and feathers. Sometimes I bind it together with spider silk, and if you really want to know, I like a little hemlock-tree to put it in. It isn't very far from here, but where it is I'm not going to tell you. Have you seen my cousin, Weechi?"

"No," replied Peter. "Is he anywhere around here?"

"Right here," replied another voice and Weechi the Magnolia Warbler dropped down on the ground for just a second right in front of Peter.

The top of his head and the back of his neck were gray. Above his eye was a white stripe and his cheeks were black. His throat was clear yellow, just below which was a black band. From this black streaks ran down across his yellow breast. At the root of his tail he was yellow. His tail was mostly black on top and white underneath.

His wings were black and gray with two white bars. He was a little smaller than Fidget the Myrtle Warbler and quite as restless.

Peter fairly itched to ask Weechi where his nest was, but by this time he had learned a lesson, so wisely kept his tongue still.

"What were you fellows talking about?" asked Weechi.

"Nests," replied Fidget. "I've just been telling Peter that while Cousin Sprite may like to build in that hanging moss down there, it wouldn't suit me at all."

"Nor me either," declared Weechi promptly. "I prefer to build a real nest just as you do. By the way, Fidget, I stopped to look at your nest this morning. I find we build a good deal alike and we like the same sort of a place to put it. I suppose you know that I am a rather near neighbor of yours?"

"Of course I know it," replied Fidget. "In fact I watched you start your nest. Don't you think you have it rather near the ground?"

"Not too near, Fidget; not too near. I am not as high-minded as some people. I like to be within two or three feet of the ground."

"I do myself," replied Fidget.

Fidget and Weechi became so interested in discussing nests and the proper way of building them they quite forgot Peter Rabbit. Peter sat around for a while listening, but being more interested in seeing those nests than hearing about them, he finally stole away to look for them.

He looked and looked, but there were so many young hemlock-trees and they looked so much alike that finally Peter lost patience and gave it up as a bad job.

XXVII. A New Friend and an Old One.

Peter Rabbit never will forget the first time he caught a glimpse of Glory the Cardinal, sometimes called Redbird. He had come up to the Old Orchard for his usual morning visit and just as he hopped over the old stone wall he heard a beautiful clear, loud whistle which drew his eyes to the top of an apple-tree. Peter stopped short with a little gasp of sheer astonishment and delight. Then he rubbed his eyes and looked again. He couldn't quite believe that he saw what he thought he saw. He hadn't supposed that any one, even among the feathered folks, could be quite so beautiful.

The stranger was dressed all in red, excepting a little black around the base of his bill. Even his bill was red. He wore a beautiful red crest which made him still more distinguished looking, and how he could sing! Peter had noticed that quite often the most beautifully dressed birds have the poorest songs. But this stranger's song was as beautiful as his coat, and that was one of the most beautiful, if not the most beautiful, that Peter ever had seen. Of course he lost no time in hunting up Jenny Wren. "Who is it, Jenny? Who is that beautiful stranger with such a lovely song?" cried Peter, as soon as he caught sight of Jenny.

"It's Glory the Cardinal," replied Jenny Wren promptly. "Isn't he the loveliest thing you've ever seen? I do hope he is going to stay here. As I said before, I don't often envy any one's fine clothes, but when I see Glory I'm sometimes tempted to be envious. If I were Mrs. Cardinal I'm afraid I should be jealous. There she is in the very same tree with him. Did you ever see such a difference?"

Peter looked eagerly. Instead of the glorious red of Glory,

GLORY THE CARDINAL. The is often called Redbird. you cannot mistake him.
KITTY THE CATBIRD. His black crown and slaty-gray coat make him easy to recognize.

Mrs. Cardinal wore a very dull dress. Her back was a brownish-gray. Her throat was a grayish-black. Her breast was a dull buff with a faint tinge of red. Her wings and tail were tinged with dull red. Altogether she was very soberly dressed, but a trim, neat looking little person. But if she wasn't handsomely dressed she could sing. In fact she was almost as good a singer as her handsome husband.

"I've noticed," said Peter, "that people with fine clothes spend most of their time thinking about them and are of very little use when it comes to real work in life."

"Well, you needn't think that of Glory," declared Jenny in her vigorous way. "He's just as fine as he is handsome. He's a model husband. If they make their home around here you'll find him doing his full share in the care of their babies. Sometimes they raise two families. When they do that, Glory takes charge of the first lot of youngsters as soon as they are able to leave the nest so that Mrs. Cardinal has nothing to worry about while she is sitting on the second lot of eggs. He fusses over them as if they were the only children in the world. Everybody loves Glory. Excuse me, Peter, I'm going over to find out if they are really going to stay."

When Jenny returned she was so excited she couldn't keep still a minute. "They like here, Peter!" she cried. "They like here so much that if they can find a place to suit them for a nest they're going to stay. I told them that it is the very best place in the world. They like an evergreen tree to build in, and I think they've got their eyes on those evergreens up near Farmer Brown's house. My, they will add a lot to the quality of this neighborhood."

Mr. and Mrs. Cardinal whistled and sang as if their hearts were bursting with joy, and Peter sat around listening as if he had nothing else in the world to do. Probably he would have sat there the rest of the morning had he not caught sight of an old friend of whom he is very fond, Kitty the Catbird. In contrast with Glory, Kitty seemed a regular little Quaker, for he was dressed almost wholly in gray, a rather dark, slaty-gray. The top of his head and tail were black, and right at the base of his tail was a patch of chestnut color. He was a little smaller than Welcome

Robin. There was no danger of mistaking him for anybody else, for there is no one dressed at all like him.

Peter forgot all about Glory in his pleasure at discovering the returned Kitty and hurried over to welcome him. Kitty had disappeared among the bushes along the old stone wall, but Peter had no trouble in finding him by the queer cries he was uttering, which were very like the meow of Black Pussy the Cat. They were very harsh and unpleasant and Peter understood perfectly why their maker is called the Catbird. He did not hurry in among the bushes at once but waited expectantly. In a few minutes the harsh cries ceased and then there came from the very same place a song which seemed to be made up of parts of the songs of all the other birds of the Old Orchard. It was not loud, but it was charming. It contained the clear whistle of Glory, and there was even the tinkle of Little Friend the Song Sparrow. The notes of other friends were in that song, and with them were notes of southern birds whose songs Kitty had learned while spending the winter in the South. Then there were notes all his own.

Peter listened until the song ended, then scampered in among the bushes. At once those harsh cries broke out again. You would have thought that Kitty was scolding Peter for coming to see him instead of being glad. But that was just Kitty's way. He is simply brimming over with fun and mischief, and delights to pretend.

When Peter found him, he was sitting with all his feathers puffed out until he looked almost like a ball with a head and tail. He looked positively sleepy. Then as he caught sight of Peter he drew those feathers down tight, cocked his tail up after the manner of Jenny Wren, and was as slim and trim looking as any bird of Peter's acquaintance. He didn't look at all like the same bird of the moment before. Then he dropped his tail as if he hadn't strength enough to hold it up at all. It hung straight down. He dropped his wings and all in a second made himself look fairly disreputable. But all the time his eyes were twinkling and snapping, and Peter knew that these changes in appearance were made out of pure fun and mischief.

"I've been wondering if you were coming back," cried Peter. "I don't know of any one of my feathered friends I would miss so much as you."

"Thank you," responded Kitty. "It's very nice of you to say that, Peter. If you are glad to see me I am still more glad to get back."

"Did you pass a pleasant winter down South?" asked Peter.

"Fairly so. Fairly so," replied Kitty. "By the way, Peter, I picked up some new songs down there. Would you like to hear them?"

"Of course," replied Peter, "but I don't think you need any new songs. I've never seen such a fellow for picking up other people's songs excepting Mocker the Mockingbird."

At the mention of Mocker a little cloud crossed Kitty's face for just an instant. "There's a fellow I really envy," said he. "I'm pretty good at imitating others, but Mocker is better. I'm hoping that, if I practice enough, some day I can be as good. I saw a lot of him in the South and he certainly is clever."

"Huh! You don't need to envy him," retorted Peter. "You are some imitator yourself. How about those new notes you got when you were in the South?"

Kitty's face cleared, his throat swelled and he began to sing. It was a regular medley. It didn't seem as if so many notes could come from one throat. When it ended Peter had a question all ready.

"Are you going to build somewhere near here?" he asked.

"I certainly am," replied Kitty. "Mrs. Catbird was delayed a day or two. I hope she'll get here to-day and then we'll get busy at once. I think we shall build in these bushes here somewhere. I'm glad Farmer Brown has sense enough to let them grow. They are just the kind of a place I like for a nest. They are near enough to Farmer Brown's garden, and the Old Orchard is right here. That's just the kind of a combination that suits me."

Peter looked somewhat uncertain. "Why do you want to be near Farmer Brown's garden?" he asked.

"Because that is where I will get a good part of my living," Kitty responded promptly. "He ought to be glad to have me about. Once in a while I take a little fruit, but I pay for it ten times over by the number of bugs and worms I get in his garden and the Old Orchard. I pride myself on being useful. There's nothing like being useful in this world, Peter."

Peter nodded as if he quite agreed. Though, as you know and I know, Peter himself does very little except fill his own big stomach.

XXVIII. Peter Sees Rosebreast and Finds Redcoat.

"WHO'S THAT?" Peter Rabbit pricked up his long ears and stared up at the tops of the trees of the Old Orchard.

Instantly Jenny Wren popped her head out of her doorway. She cocked her head on one side to listen, then looked down at Peter, and her sharp little eyes snapped.

"I don't hear any strange voice," said she. "The way you are staring, Peter Rabbit, one would think that you had really heard something new and worth while."

Just then there were two or three rather sharp, squeaky notes from the top of one of the trees. "There!" cried Peter. "There! Didn't you hear that, Jenny Wren?"

"For goodness' sake, Peter Rabbit, you don't mean to say you don't know whose voice that is," she cried. "That's Rosebreast. He and Mrs. Rosebreast have been here for quite a little while. I didn't suppose there was any one who didn't know those sharp, squeaky voices. They rather get on my nerves. What anybody wants to squeak like that for when they can sing as Rosebreast can, is more than I can understand."

At that very instant Mr. Wren began to scold as only he and Jenny can. Peter looked up at Jenny and winked slyly. "And what anybody wants to scold like that for when they can sing as Mr. Wren can, is too much for me," retorted Peter. "But you haven't told me who Rosebreast is."

"The Grosbeak, of course, stupid," sputtered Jenny. "If you don't know Rosebreast the Grosbeak, Peter Rabbit, you certainly must have been blind and deaf ever since you were born. Listen to that! Just listen to that song!"

Peter listened. There were many songs, for it was a very

beautiful morning and all the singers of the Old Orchard were pouring out the joy that was within them. One song was a little louder and clearer than the others because it came from a tree very close at hand, the very tree from which those squeaky notes had come just a few minutes before. Peter suspected that that must be the song Jenny Wren meant. He looked puzzled. He was puzzled. "Do you mean Welcome Robin's song?" he asked rather sheepishly, for he had a feeling that he would be the victim of Jenny Wren's sharp tongue.

"No, I don't mean Welcome Robin's song," snapped Jenny. "What good are a pair of long ears if they can't tell one song from another? That song may sound something like Welcome Robin's, but if your ears were good for anything at all you'd know right away that that isn't Welcome Robin singing. That's a better song than Welcome Robin's. Welcome Robin's song is one of good cheer, but this one is of pure happiness. I wouldn't have a pair of ears like yours for anything in the world, Peter Rabbit."

Peter laughed right out as he tried to picture to himself Jenny Wren with a pair of long ears like his. "What are you laughing at?" demanded Jenny crossly. "Don't you dare laugh at me! If there is any one thing I can't stand it is being laughed at."

"I wasn't laughing at you," replied Peter very meekly. "I was just laughing, at the thought of how funny you would look with a pair of long ears like mine. Now you speak of it, Jenny, that song *is* quite different from Welcome Robin's."

"Of course it is," retorted Jenny. "That is Rosebreast singing up there, and there he is right in the top of that tree. Isn't he handsome?"

Peter looked up to see a bird a little smaller than Welcome Robin. His head, throat and back were black. His wings were black with patches of white on them. But it was his breast that made Peter catch his breath with a little gasp of admiration, for that breast was a beautiful rose-red. The rest of him underneath was white. It was Rosebreast the Grosbeak.

"Isn't he lovely!"' cried Peter, and added in the next breath, "Who is that with him?"

"Mrs. Grosbeak, of course. Who else would it be?" sputtered Jenny rather crossly, for she was still a little put out because

REDCOAT THE SCARLET TANAGER. He is all red save his black wings and tail.

ROSEBREAST THE GROSBEAK. You cannot mistake this black and white bird with the rose colored breast for any one else. It is the Rosebreasted Grosbeak.

she had been laughed at.

"I would never have guessed it," said Peter. "She doesn't look the least bit like him."

This was quite true. There was no beautiful rose color about Mrs. Grosbeak. She was dressed chiefly in brown and grayish colors with a little buff here and there and with dark streaks on her breast. Over each eye was a whitish line. Altogether she looked more as if she might be a big member of the Sparrow family than the wife of handsome Rosebreast. While Rosebreast sang, Mrs. Grosbeak was very busily picking buds and blossoms from the tree.

"What is she doing that for?" inquired Peter.

"For the same reason that you bite off sweet clover blossoms and leaves," replied Jenny Wren tartly.

"Do you mean to say that they live on buds and blossoms?" cried Peter. "I never heard of such a thing."

"Tut, tut, tut, tut, tut! You can ask more silly questions than anybody of my acquaintance," retorted Jenny Wren. "Of course they don't live on buds and blossoms. If they did they would soon starve to death, for buds and blossoms don't last long. They eat a few just for variety, but they live mostly on bugs and insects. You ask Farmer Brown's boy who helps him most in his potato patch, and he'll tell you it's the Grosbeaks. They certainly do love potato bugs. They eat some fruit, but on the whole they are about as useful around a garden as any one I know. Now run along, Peter Rabbit, and don't bother me any more."

Seeing Farmer Brown's boy coming through the Old Orchard Peter decided that it was high time for him to depart. So he scampered for the Green Forest, lipperty-lipperty-lip. Just within the edge of the Green Forest he caught sight of something which for the time being put all thought of Farmer Brown's boy out of his head. Fluttering on the ground was a bird than whom not even Glory the Cardinal was more beautiful. It was about the size of Redwing the Blackbird. Wings and tail were pure black and all the rest was a beautiful scarlet. It was Redcoat the Tanager. At first Peter had eyes only for the wonderful beauty of Redcoat. Never before had he seen Redcoat so close at hand. Then quite suddenly it came over Peter that something was wrong with Redcoat, and he hurried forward to see what the trouble might be.

Redcoat heard the rustle of Peter's feet among the dry leaves and at once began to flap and flutter in an effort to fly away, but he could not get off the ground. "What is it, Redcoat? Has something happened to you? It is just Peter Rabbit. You don't have anything to fear from me," cried Peter.

The look of terror which had been in the eyes of Redcoat died out, and he stopped fluttering and simply lay panting.

"Oh, Peter," he gasped, "you don't know how glad I am that it is only you. I've had a terrible accident, and I don't know what I am to do. I can't fly, and if I have to stay on the ground some enemy will be sure to get me. What shall I do, Peter? What shall I do?"

Right away Peter was full of sympathy. "What kind of an accident was it, Redcoat, and how did it happen?" he asked.

"Broadwing the Hawk tried to catch me," sobbed Redcoat. "In dodging him among the trees I was heedless for a moment and did not see just where I was going. I struck a sharp-pointed dead twig and drove it right through my right wing."

Redcoat held up his right wing and sure enough there was a little stick projecting from both sides close up to the shoulder. The wing was bleeding a little.

"Oh, dear, whatever shall I do, Peter Rabbit? Whatever shall I do?" sobbed Redcoat.

"Does it pain you dreadfully?" asked Peter.

Redcoat nodded. "But I don't mind the pain," he hastened to say. "It is the thought of what *may* happen to me."

Meanwhile Mrs. Tanager was flying about in the tree tops near at hand and calling anxiously. She was dressed almost wholly in light olive-green and greenish-yellow. She looked no more like beautiful Redcoat than did Mrs. Grosbeak like Rosebreast.

"Can't you fly up just a little way so as to get off the ground?" she cried anxiously. "Isn't it dreadful, Peter Rabbit, to have such an accident? We've just got our nest half built, and I don't know what I shall do if anything happens to Redcoat. Oh, dear, here comes somebody! Hide, Redcoat! Hide!" Mrs. Tanager flew off a short distance to one side and began to cry as if in the greatest distress. Peter knew instantly that she was crying to get the attention of whoever was coming.

Poor Redcoat, with the old look of terror in his eyes, fluttered along, trying to find something under which to hide. But there was nothing under which he could crawl, and there was no hiding that wonderful red coat. Peter heard the sound of heavy footsteps, and looking back, saw that Farmer Brown's boy was coming. "Don't be afraid, Redcoat," he whispered. "It's Farmer Brown's boy and I'm sure he won't hurt you. Perhaps he can help you." Then Peter scampered off for a short distance and sat up to watch what would happen.

Of course Farmer Brown's boy saw Redcoat. No one with any eyes at all could have helped seeing him, because of that wonderful scarlet coat. He saw, too, by the way Redcoat was acting, that he was in great trouble. As Farmer Brown's boy drew near and Redcoat saw that he was discovered, he tried his hardest to flutter away. Farmer Brown's boy understood instantly that something was wrong with one wing, and running forward, he caught Redcoat.

"You poor little thing. You poor, beautiful little creature," said Farmer Brown's boy softly as he saw the cruel twig sticking through Redcoats' shoulder. "We'll have to get that out right away," continued Farmer Brown's boy, stroking Redcoat ever so gently.

Somehow at that gentle touch Redcoat lost much of his fear, and a little hope sprang in his heart. He saw, too, this was no enemy, but a friend. Farmer Brown's boy took out his knife and carefully cut off the twig on the upper side of the wing. Then, doing his best to be careful and to hurt as little as possible, he worked the other part of the twig out from the under side. Carefully he examined the wing to see if any bones were broken. None were, and after holding Redcoat a few minutes he carefully set him up in a tree and withdrew a short distance. Redcoat hopped from branch to branch until he was halfway up the tree. Then he sat there for some time as if fearful of trying that injured wing. Meanwhile Mrs. Tanager came and fussed about him and talked to him and coaxed him and made as much of him as if he were a baby.

Peter remained right where he was until at last he saw Redcoat spread his black wings and fly to another tree. From tree to tree he flew, resting a bit in each until he and Mrs. Tanager disappeared in the Green Forest.

"I knew Farmer Brown's boy would help him, and I'm so glad he found him," cried Peter happily and started for the dear Old Briar-patch.

XXIX. The Constant Singers.

Over in a maple-tree on the edge of Farmer Brown's door yard lived Mr. and Mrs. Redeye the Vireos. Peter Rabbit knew that they had a nest there because Jenny Wren had told him so. He would have guessed it anyway, because Redeye spent so much time in that tree during the nesting season. No matter what hour of the day Peter visited the Old Orchard he heard Redeye singing over in the maple-tree. Peter used to think that if song is an expression of happiness, Redeye must be the happiest of all birds.

He was a little fellow about the size of one of the larger Warblers and quite as modestly dressed as any of Peter's acquaintances. The crown of his head was gray with a little blackish border on either side. Over each eye was a white line. Underneath he was white. For the rest he was dressed in light olive-green. The first time he came down near enough for Peter to see him well Peter understood at once why he is called Redeye. His eyes were red. Yes, sir, his eyes were red and this fact alone was enough to distinguish him from any other members of his family.

But it wasn't often that Redeye came down so near the ground that Peter could see his eyes. He preferred to spend most of his time in the tree tops, and Peter only got glimpses of him now and then. But if he didn't see him often it was less often that he failed to hear him. "I don't see when Redeye finds time to eat," declared Peter as he listened to the seemingly unending song in the maple-tree.

"Redeye believes in singing while he works," said Jenny Wren. "For my part I should think he'd wear his throat out. When other birds sing they don't do anything else, but Redeye sings all the time he is hunting his meals and only stops long enough to swallow a worm or a bug when he finds it. Just as soon as it is down he begins to sing again while he hunts for another. I must say for the Redeyes that they are mighty good nest builders. Have you seen their nest over in that maple-tree, Peter?"

Peter shook his head.

"I don't dare go over there except very early in the morning before Farmer Brown's folks are awake," said he, "so I haven't had much chance to look for it."

"You probably couldn't see it, anyway," declared Jenny Wren. "They have placed it rather high up from the ground and those leaves are so thick that they hide it. It's a regular little basket fastened in a fork near the end of a branch and it is woven almost as nicely as is the nest of Goldy the Oriole. How anybody has the patience to weave a nest like that is beyond me."

"What's it made of?" asked Peter.

"Strips of bark, plant down, spider's web, grass, and pieces of paper!" replied Jenny. "That's a funny thing about Redeye; he dearly loves a piece of paper in his nest. What for, I can't imagine. He's as fussy about having a scrap of paper as Cresty the Flycatcher is about having a piece of Snakeskin. I had just a peep into that nest a few days ago and unless I am greatly mistaken Sally Sly the Cowbird has managed to impose on the Redeyes. I am certain I saw one of her eggs in that nest."

A few mornings after this talk with Jenny Wren about Redeye the Vireo Peter once more visited the Old Orchard. No sooner did he come in sight than Jenny Wren's tongue began to fly. "What did I tell you, Peter Rabbit? What did I tell you? I knew it was so, and it is!" cried Jenny.

"What is so?" asked Peter rather testily, for he hadn't the least idea what Jenny Wren was talking about.

"Sally Sly *did* lay an egg in Redeye's nest, and now it has hatched and I don't know whatever is to become of Redeye's own children. It's perfectly scandalous! That's what it is, perfectly scandalous!" cried Jenny, and hopped about and jerked her tail and worked herself into a small brown fury.

"The Redeyes are working themselves to feathers and bone feeding that ugly young Cowbird while their own babies aren't getting half enough to eat," continued Jenny. "One of them has died already. He was kicked out of the nest by that young brute."

"How dreadful!" cried Peter. "If he does things like that I should think the Redeyes would throw *him* out of the nest."

"They're too soft-hearted," declared Jenny. "I can tell you I wouldn't be so soft-hearted if I were in their place. No, sir-ee, I wouldn't! But they say it isn't his fault that he's there, and that he's nothing but a helpless baby, and so they just take care of him."

"Then why don't they feed their own babies first and give him what's left?" demanded Peter.

"Because he's twice as big as any of their own babies and so strong and greedy that he simply snatches the food out of the very mouths of the others. Because he gets most of the food, he's growing twice as fast as they are. I wouldn't be surprised if he kicks all the rest of them out before he gets through. Mr. and Mrs. Redeye are dreadfully distressed about it, but they will feed him because they say it isn't his fault. It's a dreadful affair and the talk of the whole Orchard. I suppose his mother is off gadding somewhere, having a good time and not caring a flip of her tail feathers what becomes of him. I believe in being goodhearted, but there is such a thing as overdoing the matter. Thank goodness I'm not so weak-minded that I can be imposed on in any such way as that."

"Speaking of the Vireos, Redeye seems to be the only member of his family around here," remarked Peter.

"Listen!" commanded Jenny Wren. "Don't you hear that warbling song 'way over in the big elm in front of Farmer Brown's house where Goldy the oriole has his nest?"

Peter listened. At first he didn't hear it, and as usual Jenny Wren made fun of him for having such big ears and not being able to make better use of them. Presently he did hear it. The voice was not unlike that of Redeye, but the song was smoother, more continuous and sweeter. Peter's face lighted up. "I hear it," he cried.

"That's Redeye's cousin, the Warbling Vireo," said Jenny. "He's a better singer than Redeye and just as fond of hearing his own voice. He sings from the time jolly Mr. Sun gets up in the morning until he goes to bed at night. He sings when it is so hot that the rest of us are glad to keep still for comfort's sake. I don't know of anybody more fond of the tree tops than he is. He doesn't seem to care anything about the Old Orchard, but stays over in those big trees along the road. He's got a nest over in that big elm and it is as high up as that of Goldy the Oriole; I haven't seen it myself, but Goldy told me about it. Why any one so small should want to live so high up in the world I don't know, any more than I know why any one wants to live anywhere but in the Old Orchard."

"Somehow I don't remember just what Warble looks like," Peter confessed.

"He looks a lot like his cousin, Redeye," replied Jenny. "His coat is a little duller olive-green and underneath he is a little bit yellowish instead of being white. Of course he doesn't have red eyes, and he is a little smaller than Redeye. The whole family looks pretty much alike anyway."

"You said something then, Jenny Wren," declared Peter. "They get me all mixed up. If only some of them had some bright colors it would be easier to tell them apart."

"One has," replied Jenny Wren. "He has a bright yellow throat and breast and is called the Yellow-throated Vireo. There isn't the least chance of mistaking him."

"Is he a singer, too?" asked Peter.

"Of course," replied Jenny. "Every one of that blessed family loves the sound of his own voice. It's a family trait. Sometimes it just makes my throat sore to listen to them all day long. A good thing is good, but more than enough of a good thing is too much. That applies to gossiping just as well as to singing and I've wasted more time on you than I've any business to. Now hop along, Peter, and don't bother me any more to-day."

Peter hopped.

XXX. Jenny Wren's Cousins.

Peter Rabbit never will forget his surprise when Jenny Wren asked him one spring morning if he had seen anything of her big cousin. Peter hesitated. As a matter of fact, he couldn't think of any big cousin of Jenny Wren. All the cousins he knew anything about were very nearly Jenny's own size.

Now Jenny Wren is one of the most impatient small persons in the world. "Well, well, well, Peter, have you lost your tongue?" she chattered. "Can't you answer a simple question without talking all day about it? Have you seen anything of my big cousin? It is high time for him to be here."

"You needn't be so cross about it if I am slow," replied Peter. "I'm just trying to think who your big cousin is. I guess, to be quite honest, I don't know him."

"Don't know him! Don't know him!" Sputtered Jenny. "Of course you know him. You can't help but know him. I mean Brownie the Thrasher."

In his surprise Peter fairly jumped right off the ground. "What's that?" he exclaimed. "Since when was Brownie the Thrasher related to the Wren family?"

"Ever since there have been any Wrens and Thrashers," retorted Jenny. "Brownie belongs to one branch of the family and I belong to another, and that makes him my second cousin. It certainly is surprising how little some folks know."

"But I have always supposed he belonged to the Thrush family," protested Peter. "He certainly looks like a Thrush."

"Looking like one doesn't make him one," snapped Jenny. "By this time you ought to leave learned that you never can judge anybody just by looks. It always makes me provoked to hear Brownie called the Brown Thrush. There isn't a drop of Thrush blood in him. But you haven't answered my question yet, Peter Rabbit. I want to know if he has got here yet."

"Yes," said Peter. "I saw him only yesterday on the edge of the Old Pasture. He was fussing around in the bushes and on the ground and jerking that long tail of his up and down and sidewise as if he couldn't decide what to do with it. I've never seen anybody twitch their tail around the way he does."

Jenny Wren giggled. "That's just like him," said she. "It is because he thrashes his tail around so much that he is called a Thrasher. I suppose he was wearing his new spring suit."

"I don't know whether it was a new suit or not, but it was mighty good looking," replied Peter. "I just love that beautiful reddish-brown of his back, wings and tail, and it certainly does set off his white and buff waistcoat with those dark streaks and spots. You must admit, Jenny Wren, that any one seeing him dressed so much like the Thrushes is to be excused for thinking him a Thrush."

"I suppose so," admitted Jenny rather grudgingly. "But none of the Thrushes have such a bright brown coat. Brownie is handsome, if I do say so. Did you notice what a long bill he has?"

Peter nodded. "And I noticed that he had two white bars on each wing," said he.

"I'm glad you're so observing," replied Jenny dryly. "Did you hear him sing?"

"Did I hear him sing!" cried Peter, his eyes shining at the memory. "He sang especially for me. He flew up to the top of a tree, tipped his head back and sang as few birds I know of can sing. He has a wonderful voice, has Brownie. I don't know of anybody I enjoy listening to more. And when he's singing he acts as if he enjoyed it himself and knows what a good singer he is. I noticed that long tail of his hung straight down the same way Mr. Wren's does when he sings."

"Of course it did," replied Jenny promptly. "That's a family trait. The tails of both my other big cousins do the same thing."

"Wha-wha-what's that? Have you got more big cousins?" cried Peter, staring up at Jenny as if she were some strange person he never had seen before.

BROWNIE THE THRASHER. You cannot mistake him because of his bright reddish-brown coat, long tail and spotted breast.

CHEWINK THE TOWHEE. He is black and white with reddish-brown sides, usually on the ground in a thicket.

"Certainly," retorted Jenny. "Mocker the Mockingbird and Kitty the Catbird belong to Brownie's family, and that makes them second cousins to me."

Such a funny expression as there was on Peter's face. He felt that Jenny Wren was telling the truth, but it was surprising news to him and so hard to believe that for a few minutes he couldn't find his tongue to ask another question. Finally he ventured to ask very timidly, "Does Brownie imitate the songs of other birds the way Mocker and Kitty do?"

Jenny Wren shook her head very decidedly. "No," said she. "He's perfectly satisfied with his own song." Before she could add anything further the clear whistle of Glory the Cardinal sounded from a tree just a little way off. Instantly Peter forgot all about Jenny Wren's relatives and scampered over to that tree. You see Glory is so beautiful that Peter never loses a chance to see him.

As Peter sat staring up into the tree, trying to get a glimpse of Glory's beautiful red coat, the clear, sweet whistle sounded once more. It drew Peter's eyes to one of the upper branches, but instead of the beautiful, brilliant coat of Glory the Cardinal he saw a bird about the size of Welcome Robin dressed in sober ashy-gray with two white bars on his wings, and white feathers on the outer edges of his tail. He was very trim and neat and his tail hung straight down after the manner of Brownie's when he was singing. It was a long tail, but not as long as Brownie's. Even as Peter blinked and stared in surprise the stranger opened his mouth and from it came Glory's own beautiful whistle. Then the stranger looked down at Peter, and his eyes twinkled with mischief.

"Fooled you that time, didn't I, Peter?" he chuckled. "You thought you were going to see Glory the Cardinal, didn't you?"

Then without waiting for Peter to reply, this sober-looking stranger gave such a concert as no one else in the world could give. From that wonderful throat poured out song after song and note after note of Peter's familiar friends of the Old Orchard, and the performance wound up with a lovely song which was all the stranger's own. Peter didn't have to be told who the stranger was. It was Mocker the Mockingbird.

"Oh!" gasped Peter. "Oh, Mocker, how under the sun do

you do it? I was sure that it was Glory whom I heard whistling. Never again will I be able to believe my own ears."

Mocker chuckled. "You're not the only one I've fooled, Peter," said he. "I flatter myself that I can fool almost anybody if I set out to. It's lots of fun. I may not be much to look at, but when it comes to singing there's no one I envy.

"I think you are very nice looking indeed," replied Peter politely. "I've just been finding out this morning that you can't tell much about folks just by their looks."

"And now you've learned that you can't always recognize folks by their voices, haven't you?" chuckled Mocker.

"Yes," replied Peter. "Hereafter I shall never be sure about any feathered folks unless I can both see and hear them. Won't you sing for me again, Mocker?"

Mocker did. He sang and sang, for he clearly loves to sing. When he finished Peter had another question ready. "Somebody told me once that down in the South you are the best loved of all the birds. Is that so?"

"That's not for me to say," replied Mocker modestly. "But I can tell you this, Peter, they do think a lot of me down there. There are many birds down there who are very beautifully dressed, birds who don't come up here at all. But not one of them is loved as I am, and it is all on account of my voice. I would rather have a beautiful voice than a fine coat."

Peter nodded as if he quite agreed, which, when you think of it, is rather funny, for Peter has neither a fine coat nor a fine voice. A glint of mischief sparkled in Mocker's eyes. "There's Mrs. Goldy the Oriole over there," said he. "Watch me fool her."

He began to call in exact imitation of Goldy's voice when he is anxious about something. At once Mrs. Goldy came hurrying over to find out what the trouble was. When she discovered Mocker she lost her temper and scolded him roundly; then she flew away a perfect picture of indignation. Mocker and Peter laughed, for they thought it a good joke.

Suddenly Peter remembered what Jenny Wren had told him. "Was Jenny Wren telling you the truth when she said that you are a second cousin of hers?" he asked.

Mocker nodded. "Yes," said he, "we are relatives. We each

belong to a branch of the same family." Then he burst into Mr. Wren's own song, after which he excused himself and went to look for Mrs. Mocker. For, as he explained, it was time for them to be thinking of a nest.

XXXI. Voices of the Dusk.

Jolly, round, red Mr. Sun was just going to bed behind the Purple Hills and the Black Shadows had begun to creep all through the Green Forest and out across the Green Meadows. It was the hour of the day Peter Rabbit loves best. He sat on the edge of the Green Forest watching for the first little star to twinkle high up in the sky. Peter felt at peace with all the Great World, for it was the hour of peace, the hour of rest for those who had been busy all through the shining day.

Most of Peter's feathered friends had settled themselves for the coming night, the worries and cares of the day over and forgotten. All the Great World seemed hushed. In the distance Sweetvoice the Vesper Sparrow was pouring out his evening song, for it was the hour when he dearly loves to sing. Far back in the Green Forest Whip-poor-will was calling as if his very life depended on the number of times he could say, "Whip poor Will," without taking a breath. From overhead came now and then the sharp, rather harsh cry of Boomer the Nighthawk, as he hunted his supper in the air.

For a time it seemed as if these were the only feathered friends still awake, and Peter couldn't help thinking that those who went so early to bed missed the most beautiful hour of the whole day. Then, from a tree just back of him, there poured forth a song so clear, so sweet, so wonderfully suited to that peaceful hour, that Peter held his breath until it was finished. He knew that singer and loved him. It was Melody the Wood Thrush.

When the song ended Peter hopped over to the tree from which it had come. It was still light enough for him to see the sweet singer. He sat on a branch near the top, his head thrown

MELODY THE WOOD THRUSH. His sides are spotted like his breast.
TEACHER THE OVEN BIRD. You can tell him by the way he repeats his own name.

back and his soft, full throat throbbing with the flute-like notes he was pouring forth. He was a little smaller than Welcome Robin. His coat was a beautiful reddish-brown, not quite so bright as that of Brownie the Thrasher. Beneath he was white with large, black spots thickly dotting his breast and sides. He was singing as if he were trying to put into those beautiful notes all the joy of life. Listening to it Peter felt steal over him a wonderful feeling of peace and pure happiness. Not for the world would he have interrupted it.

The Black Shadows crept far across the Green Meadows and it became so dusky in the Green Forest that Peter could barely make out the sweet singer above his head. Still Melody sang on and the hush of eventide grew deeper, as if all the Great World were holding its breath to listen. It was not until several little stars had begun to twinkle high up in the sky that Melody stopped singing and sought the safety of his hidden perch for the night. Peter felt sure that somewhere near was a nest and that one thing which had made that song so beautiful was the love Melody had been trying to express to the little mate sitting on the eggs that nest must contain. "I'll just run over here early in the morning," thought Peter.

Now Peter is a great hand to stay out all night, and that is just what he did that night. Just before it was time for jolly, round, red Mr. Sun to kick off his rosy blankets and begin his daily climb up in the blue, blue sky, Peter started for home in the dear Old Briar-patch. Everywhere in the Green Forest, in the Old Orchard, on the Green Meadows, his feathered friends were awakening. He had quite forgotten his intention to visit Melody and was reminded of it only when again he heard those beautiful flute-like notes. At once he scampered over to where he had spent such a peaceful hour the evening before. Melody saw him at once and dropped down on the ground for a little gossip while he scratched among the leaves in search of his breakfast.

"I just love to hear you sing, Melody," cried Peter rather breathlessly. "I don't know of any other song that makes me feel quite as yours does, so sort of perfectly contented and free of care and worry."

"Thank you," replied Melody. "I'm glad you like to hear me

sing for there is nothing I like to do better. It is the one way in which I can express my feelings. I love all the Great World and I just have to tell it so. I do not mean to boast when I say that all the Thrush family have good voices."

"But you have the best of all," cried Peter.

Melody shook his brown head. "I wouldn't say that," said he modestly. "I think the song of my cousin Hermit, is even more beautiful than mine. And then there is my other cousin, Veery. His song is wonderful, I think."

But just then Peter's curiosity was greater than his interest in songs. "Have you built your nest yet?" he asked.

Melody nodded. "It is in a little tree not far from here," said he, "and Mrs. Wood Thrush is sitting on five eggs this blessed minute. Isn't that perfectly lovely?"

It was Peter's turn to nod. "What is your nest built of?" he inquired.

"Rootlets and tiny twigs and weed stalks and leaves and mud," replied Melody.

"Mud!" exclaimed Peter. "Why, that's what Welcome Robin uses in his nest."

"Well, Welcome Robin is my own cousin, so I don't know as there's anything so surprising in that," retorted Melody.

"Oh," said Peter. "I had forgotten that he is a member of the Thrush family."

"Well, he is, even if he is dressed quite differently from the rest of us," replied Melody.

"You mentioned your cousin, Hermit. I don't believe I know him," said Peter.

"Then it's high time you got acquainted with him," replied Melody promptly. "He is rather fond of being by himself and that is why he is called the Hermit Thrush. He is smaller than I and his coat is not such a bright brown. His tail is brighter than his coat. He has a waistcoat spotted very much like mine. Some folks consider him the most beautiful singer of the Thrush family. I'm glad you like my song, but you must hear Hermit sing. I really think there is no song so beautiful in all the Green Forest."

"Does he build a nest like yours?" asked Peter.

"No," replied Melody. "He builds his nest on the ground,

and he doesn't use any mud. Now if you'll excuse me, Peter, I must get my breakfast and give Mrs. Wood Thrush a chance to get hers."

So Peter continued on his way to the dear Old Briar-patch and there he spent the day. As evening approached he decided to go back to hear Melody sing again. Just as he drew near the Green Forest he heard from the direction of the Laughing Brook a song that caused him to change his mind and sent him hurrying in that direction. It was a very different song from that of Melody the Wood Thrush, yet, if he had never heard it before, Peter would have known that such a song could come from no throat except that of a member of the Thrush family. As he drew near the Laughing Brook the beautiful notes seemed to ring through the Green Forest like a bell. As Melody's song had filled Peter with a feeling of peace, so this song stirred in him a feeling of the wonderful mystery of life. There was in it the very spirit of the Green Forest.

It didn't take Peter long to find the singer. It was Veery, who has been named Wilson's Thrush; and by some folks is known as the Tawny Thrush.

At the sound of the patter of Peter's feet the song stopped abruptly and he was greeted with a whistled "Wheeu! wheeu!" Then, seeing that it was no one of whom he need be afraid, Veery came out from under some ferns to greet Peter. He was smaller than Melody the Wood Thrush, being about one-fourth smaller than Welcome Robin. He wore a brown coat but it was not as bright as that of his cousin, Melody. His breast was somewhat faintly spotted with brown, and below he was white. His sides were grayish-white and not spotted like the sides of Melody.

"I heard you singing and I just had to come over to see you," cried Peter.

"I hope you like my song," said Veery. "I love to sing just at this hour and I love to think that other people like to hear me."

"They do," declared Peter most emphatically. "I can't imagine how anybody could fail to like to hear you. I came 'way over here just to sit a while and listen. Won't you sing some more for me, Veery?"

"I certainly will, Peter," replied Veery. "I wouldn't feel that

I was going to bed right if I didn't sing until dark. There is no part of the day I love better than the evening, and the only way I can express my happiness and my love of the Green Forest and the joy of just being back here at home is by singing."

Veery slipped out of sight, and almost at once his bell-like notes began to ring through the Green Forest. Peter sat right where he was, content to just listen and feel within himself the joy of being alive and happy in the beautiful spring season which Veery was expressing so wonderfully. The Black Shadows grew blacker. One by one the little stars came out and twinkled down through the tree tops. Finally from deep in the Green Forest sounded the hunting call of Hooty the Owl. Veery's song stopped. "Good night, Peter," he called softly.

"Good night, Veery," replied Peter and hopped back towards the Green Meadows for a feast of sweet clover.

XXXII. Peter Saves a Friend and Learns Something.

Peter Rabbit sat in a thicket of young trees on the edge of the Green Forest. It was warm and Peter was feeling lazy. He had nothing in particular to do, and as he knew of no cooler place he had squatted there to doze a bit and dream a bit. So far as he knew, Peter was all alone. He hadn't seen anybody when he entered that little thicket, and though he had listened he hadn't heard a sound to indicate that he didn't have that thicket quite to himself. It was very quiet there, and though when he first entered he hadn't the least intention in the world of going to sleep, it wasn't long before he was dozing.

Now Peter is a light sleeper, as all little people who never know when they may have to run for their lives must be. By and by he awoke with a start, and he was very wide awake indeed. Something had wakened him, though just what it was he couldn't say. His long ears stood straight up as he listened with all his might for some little sound which might mean danger. His wobbly little nose wobbled very fast indeed as it tested the air for the scent of a possible enemy. Very alert was Peter as he waited.

For a few minutes he heard nothing and saw nothing. Then, near the outer edge of the thicket, he heard a great rustling of dry leaves. It must have been this that had wakened him. For just an instant Peter was startled, but only for an instant. His long ears told him at once that that noise was made by some one scratching among the leaves, and he knew that no one who did not wear feathers could scratch like that.

"Now who can that be?" thought Peter, and stole forward very softly towards the place from which the sound came. Presently, as he peeped between the stems of the young trees, he saw the brown leaves which carpeted the ground fly this way and that, and in the midst of them was an exceedingly busy person, a little smaller than Welcome Robin, scratching away for dear life. Every now and then he picked up something.

His head, throat, back and breast were black. Beneath he was white. His sides were reddish-brown. His tail was black and white, and the longer feathers of his wings were edged with white. It was Chewink the Towhee, sometimes called Ground Robin.

Peter chuckled, but it was a noiseless chuckle. He kept perfectly still, for it was fun to watch some one who hadn't the least idea that he was being watched. It was quite clear that Chewink was hungry and that under those dry leaves he was finding a good meal. His feet were made for scratching and he certainly knew how to use them. For some time Peter sat there watching. He had just about made up his mind that he would make his presence known and have a bit of morning gossip when, happening to look out beyond the edge of the little thicket, he saw something red. It was something alive, for it was moving very slowly and cautiously towards the place where Chewink was so busy and forgetful of everything but his breakfast. Peter knew that there was only one person with a coat of that color. It was Reddy Fox, and quite plainly Reddy was hoping to catch Chewink.

For a second or two Peter was quite undecided what to do. He couldn't warn Chewink without making his own presence known to Reddy Fox. Of course he could sit perfectly still and let Chewink be caught, but that was such a dreadful thought that Peter didn't consider it for more than a second or two. He suddenly thumped the ground with his feet. It was his danger signal which all his friends know. Then he turned and scampered lipperty-lipperty-lip to a thick bramble-tangle not far behind him.

At the sound of that thump Chewink instantly flew up in a little tree. Then he saw Reddy Fox and began to scold. As for Reddy, he looked over towards the bramble-tangle and snarled. "I'll get you one of these days, Peter Rabbit," said he. "I'll get you one of these days and pay you up for cheating me out of a breakfast." Without so much as a glance at Chewink, Reddy turned and trotted off, trying his best to look dignified and as if he had never entertained such a thought as trying to catch Chewink.

From his perch Chewink watched until he was sure that Reddy Fox had gone away for good. Then he called softly, "Towhee! Towhee! Chewink! Chewink! All is safe now, Peter Rabbit. Come out and talk with me and let me tell you how grateful to you I am for saving my life."

Chewink flew down to the ground and Peter crept out of the bramble-tangle. "It wasn't anything," declared Peter. "I saw Reddy and I knew you didn't, so of course I gave the alarm. You would have done the same thing for me. Do you know, Chewink, I've wondered a great deal about you."

"What have you wondered about me?" asked Chewink.

"I've wondered what family you belong to," replied Peter.

Chewink chuckled. "I belong to a big family," said he. "I belong to the biggest family among the birds. It is the Finch and Sparrow family. There are a lot of us and a good many of us don't look much alike, but still we belong to the same family. I suppose you know that Rosebreast the Grosbeak and Glory the Cardinal are members of my family."

"I didn't know it," replied Peter, "but if you say it is so I suppose it must be so. It is easier to believe than it is to believe that you are related to the Sparrows."

"Nevertheless I am," retorted Chewink.

"What were you scratching for when I first saw you?" asked Peter.

"Oh, worms and bugs that hide under the leaves," replied Chewink carelessly. "You have no idea how many of them hide under dead leaves."

"Do you eat anything else?" asked Peter.

"Berries and wild fruits in season," replied Chewink. "I'm very fond of them. They make a variety in the bill of fare."

"I've noticed that I seldom see you up in the tree tops," remarked Peter.

"I like the ground better," replied Chewink. "I spend more of my time on the ground than anywhere else."

"I suppose that means that you nest on the ground," ventured Peter.

Chewink nodded. "Of course," said he. "As a matter of fact, I've got a nest in this very thicket. Mrs. Towhee is on it right now, and I suspect she's worrying and anxious to know what happened over here when you warned me about Reddy Fox. I think I must go over and set her mind at rest."

Peter was just about to ask if he might go along and see that nest when a new voice broke in.

"What are you fellows talking about?" it demanded, and there flitted just in front of Peter a little bird the size of a Sparrow but lovelier than any Sparrow of Peter's acquaintance. At first glance he seemed to be all blue, and such a lovely bright blue. But as he paused for an instant Peter saw that his wings and tail were mostly black and that the lovely blue was brightest on his head and back. It was Indigo the Bunting.

"We were talking about our family," replied Chewink. "I was telling Peter that we belong to the largest family among the birds."

"But you didn't say anything about Indigo," interrupted Peter. "Do you mean to say that he belongs to the same family?"

"I surely do," replied Indigo. "I'm rather closely related to the Sparrow branch. Don't I look like a Sparrow?"

Peter looked at Indigo closely. "In size and shape you do," he confessed, "but just the same I should never in the world have thought of connecting you with the Sparrows."

"How about me?" asked another voice, and a little brown bird flew up beside Indigo, twitching her tail nervously. She looked very Sparrow-like indeed, so much so, that if Peter had not seen her with her handsome mate, for she was Mrs. Indigo, he certainly would have taken her for a Sparrow.

Only on her wings and tail was there any of the blue which made Indigo's coat so beautiful, and this was only a faint tinge.

"I'll have to confess that so far as you are concerned it isn't hard to think of you as related to the Sparrows," declared Peter. "Don't you sometimes wish you were as handsomely dressed as Indigo?"

Mrs. Indigo shook her head in a most decided way. "Never!" she declared. "I have worries enough raising a family as it is, but if I had a coat like his I wouldn't have a moment of peace.

You have no idea how I worry about him sometimes. You ought to be thankful, Peter Rabbit, that you haven't a coat like his. It attracts altogether too much attention."

Peter tried to picture himself in a bright blue coat and laughed right out at the mere thought, and the others joined with him. Then Indigo flew up to the top of a tall tree not far away and began to sing. It was a lively song and Peter enjoyed it thoroughly. Mrs. Indigo took this opportunity to slip away unobserved, and when Peter looked around for Chewink, he too had disappeared. He had gone to tell Mrs. Chewink that he was quite safe and that she had nothing to worry about.

XXXIII. A Royal Dresser and a Late Nester.

JENNY AND Mr. Wren were busy. If there were any busier little folks anywhere Peter Rabbit couldn't imagine who they could be. You see, everyone of those seven eggs in the Wren nest had hatched, and seven mouths are a lot to feed, especially when every morsel of food must be hunted for and carried from a distance. There was little time for gossip now. Just as soon as it was light enough to see Jenny and Mr. Wren began feeding those always hungry babies, and they kept at it with hardly time for an occasional mouthful themselves, until the Black Shadows came creeping out from the Purple Hills. Wren babies, like all other bird babies, grow very fast, and that means that each one of them must have a great deal of food every day. Each one of them often ate its own weight in food in a day and all their food had to be hunted for and when found carried back and put into the gaping little mouths. Hardly would Jenny Wren disappear in the little round doorway of her home with a caterpillar in her bill than she would hop out again, and Mr. Wren would take her place with a spider or a fly and then hurry away for something more.

Peter tried to keep count of the number of times they came and went but soon gave it up as a bad job. He began to wonder where all the worms and bugs and spiders came from, and gradually he came to have a great deal of respect for eyes sharp enough to find them so quickly. Needless to say Jenny was shorter-tempered than ever. She had no time to gossip and said so most emphatically. So at last Peter gave up the idea of trying to find out from her certain things he wanted to know, and hopped off to look for some one who was less busy. He had gone but a short distance when his attention was caught by a song so sweet and so full of little trills that he first stopped to listen, then went to look for the singer.

It didn't take long to find him, for he was sitting on the very tiptop of a fir-tree in Farmer Brown's yard. Peter didn't dare go over there, for already it was broad daylight, and he had about made up his mind that he would have to content himself with just listening to that sweet singer when the latter flew over in the Old Orchard and alighted just over Peter's head. "Hello, Peter!" he cried.

"Hello, Linnet!" cried Peter. "I was wondering who it could be who was singing like that. I ought to have known, but you see it's so long since I've heard you sing that I couldn't just remember your song. I'm so glad you came over here for I'm just dying to talk to somebody."

Linnet the Purple Finch, for this is who it was, laughed right out. "I see you're still the same old Peter," said he. "I suppose you're just as full of curiosity as ever and just as full of questions. Well, here I am, so what shall we talk about?"

"You," replied Peter bluntly. "Lately I've found out so many surprising things about my feathered friends that I want to know more. I'm trying to get it straight in my head who is related to who, and I've found out some things which have begun to make me feel that I know very little about my feathered neighbors. It's getting so that I don't dare to even guess who a person's relatives are. If you please, Linnet, what family do you belong to?"

Linnet flew down a little nearer to Peter. "Look me over, Peter," said he with twinkling eyes. "Look me over and see if you can't tell for yourself."

Peter stared solemnly at Linnet. He saw a bird of Sparrow size most of whose body was a rose-red, brightest on the head, darkest on the back, and palest on the breast. Underneath he was whitish.

His wings and tail were brownish, the outer parts of the feathers edged with rose-red. His bill was short and stout.

Before Peter could reply, Mrs. Linnet appeared. There wasn't so much as a touch of that beautiful rose-red about her. Her grayish-brown back was streaked with black, and her white breast and sides were spotted and streaked with brown. If Peter hadn't seen her with Linnet he certainly would have taken her for a Sparrow. She looked so much like one that he ventured to say, "I guess you belong to the Sparrow family."

"That's pretty close, Peter. That's pretty close," declared Linnet. "We belong to the Finch branch of the family, which makes the sparrows own cousins to us. Folks may get Mrs. Linnet mixed with some of our Sparrow cousins, but they never can mistake me. There isn't anybody else my size with a rose-red coat like mine. If you can't remember my song, which you ought to, because there is no other song quite like it, you can always tell me by the color of my coat. Hello! Here comes Cousin Chicoree. Did you ever see a happier fellow than he is? I'll venture to say that he has been having such a good time that he hasn't even yet thought of building a nest, and here half the people of the Old Orchard have grown families. I've a nest and eggs myself, but that madcap is just roaming about having a good time. Isn't that so, Chicoree?"

"Isn't what so?" demanded Chicoree the Goldfinch, perching very near to where Linnet was sitting.

"Isn't it true that you haven't even begun thinking about a nest?" demanded Linnet. Chicoree flew down in the grass almost under Peter's nose and began to pull apart a dandelion which had gone to seed. He snipped the seeds from the soft down to which they were attached and didn't say a word till he was quite through. Then he flew up in the tree near Linnet, and while he dressed his feathers, answered Linnet's question.

"It's quite true, but what of it?" said he. "There's time enough to think about nest-building and household cares later. Mrs. Goldfinch and I will begin to think about them about the first of July. Meanwhile we are making the most of this beautiful season to roam about and have a good time. For one thing we like thistledown to line our nest, and there isn't any thistledown yet. Then, there is no sense in raising a family until there is plenty of the right kind of food, and you know we Goldfinches live mostly on seeds. I'll venture to say that we are the greatest seed-eaters anywhere around. Of course when the babies are small they have to have soft food, but one can find plenty of

CHICOREE THE GOLDFINCH. There is no mistaking this little yellow and black bird.

HUMMER THE RUBY-THROATED HUMMINGBIRD. The only member of his family in the East.

worms and bugs any time during the summer. Just as soon as the children are big enough to hunt their own food they need seeds, so there is no sense in trying to raise a family until there are plenty of seeds for them when needed. Meanwhile we are having a good time. How do you like my summer suit, Peter?"

"It's beautiful," cried Peter. "I wouldn't know you for the same bird I see so often in the late fall and sometimes in the winter. I don't know of anybody who makes a more complete change. That black cap certainly is very smart and becoming."

Chicoree cocked his head on one side, the better to show off that black cap. The rest of his head and his whole body were bright yellow. His wings were black with two white bars on each. His tail also was black, with some white on it. In size he was a little smaller than Linnet and altogether one of the smartest appearing of all the little people who wear feathers. It was a joy just to look at him. If Peter had known anything about Canaries, which of course he didn't, because Canaries are always kept in cages, he would have understood why Chicoree the Goldfinch is often called the Wild Canary.

Mrs. Goldfinch now joined her handsome mate and it was plain to see that she admired him quite as much as did Peter. Her wings and tail were much like his but were more brownish than black. She wore no cap at all and her back and head were a grayish-brown with an olive tinge. Underneath she was lighter, with a tinge of yellow. All together she was a very modestly dressed small person. As Peter recalled Chicoree's winter suit, it was very much like that now worn by Mrs. Goldfinch, save that his wings and tail were as they now appeared.

All the time Chicoree kept up a continual happy twittering, breaking out every few moments into song. It was clear that he was fairly bubbling over with joy.

"I suppose," said Peter, "it sounds foolish of me to ask if you are a member of the same family as Linnet."

"Very foolish, Peter. Very foolish," laughed Chicoree. "Isn't my name Goldfinch, and isn't his name Purple Finch? We belong to the same family and a mighty fine family it is. Now I must go over to the Old Pasture to see how the thistles are coming on."

Away he flew calling, "Chic-o-ree, per-chic-o-ree, chic-o-ree!"

Mrs. Goldfinch followed. As they flew, they rose and fell in the air in very much the same way that Yellow Wing the Flicker does.

"I'd know them just by that, even if Chicoree didn't keep calling his own name," thought Peter. "It's funny how they often stay around all winter yet are among the last of all the birds to set up housekeeping. As I once said to Jenny Wren, birds certainly are funny creatures."

"Tut, tut, tut, tut, tut! It's no such thing, Peter Rabbit. It's no such thing," scolded Jenny Wren as she flew past Peter on her way to hunt for another worm for her hungry babies.

XXXIV. Mourner the Dove and Cuckoo.

A long lane leads from Farmer Brown's barnyard down to his cornfield on the Green Meadows. It happened that very early one morning Peter Rabbit took it into his funny little head to run down that long lane to see what he might see. Now at a certain place beside that long lane was a gravelly bank into which Farmer Brown had dug for gravel to put on the roadway up near his house. As Peter was scampering past this place where Farmer Brown had dug he caught sight of some one very busy in that gravel pit. Peter stopped short, then sat up to stare.

It was Mourner the Dove whom Peter saw, an old friend of whom Peter is very fond. His body was a little bigger than that of Welcome Robin, but his long slender neck, and longer tail and wings made him appear considerably larger. In shape he reminded Peter at once of the Pigeons up at Farmer Brown's. His back was grayish-brown, varying to bluish-gray. The crown and upper parts of his head were bluish-gray. His breast was reddish-buff, shading down into a soft buff. His bill was black and his feet red. The two middle feathers of his tail were longest and of the color of his back. The other feathers were slaty-gray with little black bands and tipped with white. On his wings were a few scattered black spots. Just under each ear was a black spot. But it was the sides of his slender neck which were the most beautiful part of Mourner. When untouched by the Jolly Little Sunbeams the neck feathers appeared to be in color very like his breast, but the moment they were touched by the Jolly Little Sunbeams they seemed to be constantly changing, which, as you know, is called iridescence. Altogether Mourner was lovely in a quiet way.

But it was not his appearance which made Peter stare; it was what he was doing. He was walking about and every now and then picking up something quite as if he were getting his breakfast in that gravel pit, and Peter couldn't imagine anything good to eat down there. He knew that there were not even worms there. Besides, Mourner is not fond of worms; he lives almost altogether on seeds and grains of many kinds. So Peter was puzzled. But as you know he isn't the kind to puzzle long over anything when he can use his tongue.

"Hello, Mourner!" he cried. "What under the sun are you doing in there? Are you getting your breakfast?"

"Hardly, Peter; hardly," cooed Mourner in the softest of voices. "I've had my breakfast and now I'm picking up a little gravel for my digestion." He picked up a tiny pebble and swallowed it.

"Well, of all things!" cried Peter. "You must be crazy. The idea of thinking that gravel is going to help your digestion. I should say the chances are that it will work just the other way."

Mourner laughed. It was the softest of little cooing laughs, very pleasant to hear. "I see that as usual you are judging others by yourself," said he. "You ought to know by this time that you can do nothing more foolish. I haven't the least doubt that a breakfast of gravel would give you the worst kind of a stomach-ache. But you are you and I am I, and there is all the difference in the world. You know I eat grain and hard seeds. Not having any teeth I have to swallow them whole. One part of my stomach is called a gizzard and its duty is to grind and crush my food so that it may be digested. Tiny pebbles and gravel help grind the food and so aid digestion. I think I've got enough now for this morning, and it is time for a dust bath. There is a dusty spot over in the lane where I take a dust bath every day."

"If you don't mind," said Peter, "I'll go with you."

Mourner said he didn't mind, so Peter followed him over to the dusty place in the long lane. There Mourner was joined by Mrs. Dove, who was dressed very much like him save that she did not have so beautiful a neck. While they thoroughly dusted themselves they chatted with Peter.

"I see you on the ground so much that I've often wondered if you build your nest on the ground," said Peter.

MOURNER THE DOVE. You may surprise him taking a dust bath in the road.

"No," replied Mourner. "Mrs. Dove builds in a tree, but usually not very far above the ground. Now if you'll excuse us we must get back home. Mrs. Dove has two eggs to sit on and while she is siting I like to be close at hand to keep her company and make love to her."

The Doves shook the loose dust from their feathers and flew away. Peter watched to see where they went, but lost sight of them behind some trees, so decided to run up to the Old Orchard. There he found Jenny and Mr. Wren as busy as ever feeding that growing family of theirs. Jenny wouldn't stop an instant to gossip. Peter was so brimful of what he had found out about Mr. and Mrs. Dove that he just had to tell some one. He heard Kitty the Catbird meowing among the bushes along the old stone wall, so hurried over to look for him. As soon as he found him Peter began to tell what he had learned about Mourner the Dove.

"That's no news, Peter," interrupted Kitty. "I know all about Mourner and his wife. They are very nice people, though I must say Mrs. Dove is one of the poorest housekeepers I know of. I take it you never have seen her nest."

Peter shook his head. "No," said he, "I haven't. What is it like?"

Kitty the Catbird laughed. "It's about the poorest apology for a nest I know of," said he. "It is made of little sticks and mighty few of them. How they hold together is more than I can understand. I guess it is a good thing that Mrs. Dove doesn't lay more than two eggs, and it's a wonder to me that those two stay in the nest. Listen! There's Mourner's voice now. For one who is so happy he certainly does have the mournfullest sounding voice. To hear him you'd think he was sorrowful instead of happy. It always makes me feel sad to hear him."

"That's true," replied Peter, "but I like to hear him just the same. Hello! Who's that?"

From one of the trees in the Old Orchard sounded a long, clear, "Kow-kow-kow-kow-kow-kow!" It was quite unlike any voice Peter had heard that spring.

"That's Cuckoo," said Kitty. "Do you mean to say you don't know Cuckoo?"

"Of course I know him," retorted Peter. "I had forgotten the sound of his voice, that's all. Tell me, Kitty, is it true that Mrs. Cuckoo is no better than Sally Sly the Cowbird and goes about laying her eggs in the nests of other birds? I've heard that said of her."

"There isn't a word of truth in it," declared Kitty emphatically. "She builds a nest, such as it is, which isn't much, and she looks after her own children. The Cuckoos have been given a bad name because of some good-for-nothing cousins of theirs who live across the ocean where Bully the English Sparrow belongs, and who, if all reports are true, really are no better than Sally Sly the Cowbird. It's funny how a bad name sticks. The Cuckoos have been accused of stealing the eggs of us other birds, but I've never known them to do it and I've lived neighbor to them for a long time, I guess they get their bad name because of their habit of slipping about silently and keeping out of sight as much as possible, as if they were guilty of doing something wrong and trying to keep from being seen. As a matter of fact, they are mighty useful birds. Farmer Brown ought to be tickled to death that Mr. and Mrs. Cuckoo have come back to the Old Orchard this year."

"Why?" demanded Peter.

"Do you see that cobwebby nest with all those hairy caterpillars on it and around it up in that tree?" asked Kitty.

Peter replied that he did and that he had seen a great many nests just like it, and had noticed how the caterpillars ate all the leaves near them.

"I'll venture to say that you won't see very many leaves eaten around that nest," replied Kitty. "Those are called tent-caterpillars, and they do an awful lot of damage. I can't bear them myself because they are so hairy, and very few birds will touch them. But Cuckoo likes them. There he comes now; just watch him."

A long, slim Dove-like looking bird alighted close to the caterpillar's nest. Above he was brownish-gray with just a little greenish tinge. Beneath he was white. His wings were reddish-brown. His tail was a little longer than that of Mourner the Dove. The outer feathers were black tipped with white, while the middle feathers were the color of his back. The upper half of his bill was black, but the under half was yellow, and from this he is called the Yellow-billed Cuckoo. He has a cousin very much like himself in appearance, save that his bill is all black and he is listed the Black-billed Cuckoo.

Cuckoo made no sound but began to pick off the hairy caterpillars and swallow them. When he had eaten all those in sight he made holes in the silken web of the nest and picked out the caterpillars that were inside. Finally, having eaten his fill, he flew off as silently as he had come and disappeared among the bushes farther along the old stone wall. A moment later they heard his voice, "Kow-kow-how-kow-kow-kow-kow-kow!"

"I suppose some folks would think that it is going to rain," remarked Kitty the Catbird. "They have the silly notion that Cuckoo only calls just before rain, and so they call him the Rain Crow. But that isn't so at all. Well, Peter, I guess I've gossiped enough for one morning. I must go see how Mrs. Catbird is getting along."

Kitty disappeared and Peter, having no one to talk to, decided that the best thing he could do would be to go home to the dear Old Briar-patch.

XXXV. A Butcher and a Hummer.

Not far from the Old Orchard grew a thorn-tree which Peter Rabbit often passed. He never had paid particular attention to it. One morning he stopped to rest under it. Happening to look up, he saw a most astonishing thing. Fastened on the sharp thorns of one of the branches were three big grasshoppers, a big moth, two big caterpillars, a lizard, a small mouse and a young English Sparrow. Do you wonder that Peter thought he must be dreaming? He couldn't imagine how those creatures could have become fastened on those long sharp thorns. Somehow it gave him an uncomfortable feeling and he hurried on to the Old Orchard, bubbling over with desire to tell some one of the strange and dreadful thing he had seen in the thorn-tree.

As he entered the Old Orchard in the far corner he saw Johnny Chuck sitting on his doorstep and hurried over to tell him the strange news. Johnny listened until Peter was through, then told him quite frankly that never had he heard of such a thing, and that he thought Peter must have been dreaming and didn't know it.

"You're wrong, Johnny Chuck. Peter hasn't been dreaming at all," said Skimmer the Swallow, who, you remember, lived in a hole in a tree just above the entrance to Johnny Chuck's house. He had been sitting where he could hear all that Peter had said.

"Well, if you know so much about it, please explain," said Johnny Chuck rather crossly.

"It's simple enough," replied Skimmer. "Peter just happened to find the storehouse of Butcher the Loggerhead Shrike. It isn't a very pleasant sight, I must admit, but one must give Butcher credit for being smart enough to lay up a store of food when it

BUTCHER THE NORTHERN SHRIKE. His cousin, the Loggerhead Shrike looks much like him.

SNIPPER THE CROSSBILL. No other bird has the tips of his bill crossed.

is plentiful."

"And who is Butcher the Shrike?" demanded Peter. "He's a new one to me.

"He's new to this location," replied Skimmer, "and you probably haven't noticed him. I've seen him in the South often. There he is now, on the tiptop of that tree over yonder."

Peter and Johnny looked eagerly. They saw a bird who at first glance appeared not unlike Mocker the Mockingbird. He was dressed wholly in black, gray and white. When he turned his head they noticed a black stripe across the side of his face and that the tip of his bill was hooked. These are enough to make them forget that otherwise he was like Mocker. While they were watching him he flew down into the grass and picked up a grasshopper. Then he flew with a steady, even flight, only a little above the ground, for some distance, suddenly shooting up and returning to the perch where they had first seen him. There he ate the grasshopper and resumed his watch for something else to catch.

"He certainly has wonderful eyes," said Skimmer admiringly. "He must have seen that grasshopper way over there in the grass before he started after it, for he flew straight there. He doesn't waste time and energy hunting aimlessly. He sits on a high perch and watches until he sees something he wants. Many times I've seen him sitting on top of a telegraph pole. I understand that Bully the English Sparrow has become terribly nervous since the arrival of Butcher. He is particularly fond of English Sparrows. I presume it was one of Bully's children you saw in the thorn-tree, Peter. For my part I hope he'll frighten Bully into leaving the Old Orchard. It would be a good thing for the rest of us."

"But I don't understand yet why he fastens his victims on those long thorns," said Peter.

"For two reasons," replied Skimmer. "When he catches more grasshoppers and other insects than he can eat, he sticks them on those thorns so that later he may be sure of a good meal if it happens there are no more to be caught when he is hungry. Mice, Sparrows, and things too big for him to swallow he sticks on the thorns so that he can pull them to pieces easier.

You see his feet and claws are not big and stout enough to hold his victims while he tears them to pieces with his hooked bill. Sometimes, instead of sticking them on thorns, he sticks them on the barbed wire of a fence and sometimes he wedges them into the fork of two branches."

"Does he kill many birds?" asked Peter.

"Not many," replied Skimmer, "and most of those he does kill are English Sparrows. The rest of us have learned to keep out of his way. He feeds mostly on insects, worms and caterpillars, but he is very fond of mice and he catches a good many. He is a good deal like Killy the Sparrow Hawk in this respect. He has a cousin, the Great Northern Shrike, who sometimes comes down in the winter, and is very much like him. Hello! Now what's happened?"

A great commotion had broken out not far away in the Old Orchard. Instantly Skimmer flew over to see what it was all about and Peter followed. He got there just in time to see Chatterer the Red Squirrel dodging around the trunk of a tree, first on one side, then on the other, to avoid the sharp bills of the angry feathered folk who had discovered him trying to rob a nest of its young.

Peter chuckled. "Chatterer is getting just what is due him, I guess," he muttered. "It reminds me of the time I got into a Yellow Jacket's nest. My, but those birds are mad!"

Chatterer continued to dodge from side to side of the tree while the birds darted down at him, all screaming at the top of their voices. Finally Chatterer saw his chance to run for the old stone wall. Only one bird was quick enough to catch up with him and that one was such a tiny fellow that he seemed hardly bigger than a big insect. It was Hammer the Hummingbird. He followed Chatterer clear to the old stone wall. A moment later Peter heard a humming noise just over his head and looked up to see Hummer himself alight on a twig, where he squeaked excitedly for a few minutes, for his voice is nothing but a little squeak.

Often Peter had seen Hummer darting about from flower to flower and holding himself still in mid-air in front of each as he thrust his long bill into the heart of the blossom to get the tiny insects there and the sweet juices he is so fond of. But this was the first time Peter had ever seen him sitting still. He was such a mite of a thing that it was hard to realize that he was a bird. His back was a bright, shining green. His wings and tail were brownish with a purplish tinge. Underneath he was whitish. But it was his throat on which Peter fixed his eyes. It was a wonderful ruby-red that glistened and shone in the sun like a jewel.

Hummer lifted one wing and with his long needle-like bill smoothed the feathers under it. Then he darted out into the air, his wings moving so fast that Peter couldn't see them at all. But if he couldn't see them he could hear them. You see they moved so fast that they made a sound very like the humming of Bumble the Bee. It is because of this that he is called the Hummingbird. A few minutes later he was back again and now he was joined by Mrs. Hummer. She was dressed very much like Hummer but did not have the beautiful ruby throat. She stopped only a minute or two, then darted over to what looked for all the world like a tiny cup of moss. It was their nest.

Just then Jenny Wren came along, and being quite worn out with the work of feeding her seven babies, she was content to rest for a few moments and gossip. Peter told her what he had discovered.

"I know all about that," retorted Jenny. "You don't suppose I hunt these trees over for food without knowing where my neighbors are living, do you? I'd have you to understand, Peter, that that is the daintiest nest in the Old Orchard. It is made wholly of plant down and covered on the outside with bits of that gray moss-like stuff that grows on the bark of the trees and is called lichens. That is what makes that nest look like nothing more than a knot on the branch. Chatterer made a big mistake when he visited this tree. Hummer may be a tiny fellow but he isn't afraid of anybody under the sun. That bill of his is so sharp and he is so quick that few folks ever bother him more than once. Why, there isn't a single member of the Hawk family that Hummer won't attack. There isn't a cowardly feather on him."

"Does he go very far south for the winter?" asked Peter. "He is such a tiny fellow I don't see how he can stand a very long journey."

"Huh!" exclaimed Jenny Wren. "Distance doesn't bother Hummer any. You needn't worry about those wings of his. He goes clear down to South America. He has ever so many relatives down there. You ought to see his babies when they first hatch out. They are no bigger than bees. But they certainly do grow fast. Why, they are flying three weeks from the time they hatch. I'm glad I don't have to pump food down the throats of my youngsters the way Mrs. Hummingbird has to down hers."

Peter looked perplexed. "What do you mean by pumping food down their throats?" he demanded.

"Just what I say," retorted Jenny Wren. "Mrs. Hummer sticks her bill right down their throats and then pumps up the food she has already swallowed. I guess it is a good thing that the babies have short bills."

"Do they?" asked Peter, opening his eyes very wide with surprise.

"Yes," replied Jenny. "When they hatch out they have short bills, but it doesn't take them a great while to grow long."

"How many babies does Mrs. Hummer usually have?" asked Peter.

"Just two," replied Jenny. "Just two. That's all that nest will hold. But goodness gracious, Peter, I can't stop gossiping here any longer. You have no idea what a care seven babies are."

With a jerk of her tail off flew Jenny Wren, and Peter hurried back to tell Johnny Chuck all he had found out about Hummer the Hummingbird.

XXXVI. A Stranger and a Dandy.

Butcher the Shrike was not the only newcomer in the Old Orchard. There was another stranger who, Peter Rabbit soon discovered, was looked on with some suspicion by all the other birds of the Old Orchard. The first time Peter saw him, he was walking about on the ground some distance off. He didn't hop but walked, and at that distance he looked all black. The way he carried himself and his movements as he walked made Peter think of Creaker the Grackle. In fact, Peter mistook him for Creaker. That was because he didn't really look at him. If he had he would have seen at once that the stranger was smaller than Creaker.

Presently the stranger flew up in a tree and Peter saw that his tail was little more than half as long as that of Creaker. At once it came over Peter that this was a stranger to him, and of course his curiosity was aroused. He didn't have any doubt whatever that this was a member of the Blackbird family, but which one it could be he hadn't the least idea. "Jenny Wren will know," thought Peter and scampered off to hunt her up.

"Who is that new member of the Blackbird family who has come to live in the Old Orchard?" Peter asked as soon as he found Jenny Wren.

"There isn't any new member of the Blackbird family living in the Old Orchard," retorted Jenny Wren tartly.

"There is too," contradicted Peter. "I saw him with my own eyes. I can see him now. He's sitting in that tree over yonder this very minute. He's all black, so of course he must be a member of the Blackbird family."

"Tut, tut, tut, tut, tut!" scolded Jenny Wren. "Tut, tut, tut, tut, tut! That fellow isn't a member of the Blackbird family at all, and what's more, he isn't black. Go over there and take a

DANDY THE CEDAR WAXWING, often called CHERRY BIRD. You can tell him from his cousin the Bohemian Waxwing by his smaller size.

good look at him; then come back and tell me if you still think he is black."

Jenny turned her back on Peter and went to hunting worms. There being nothing else to do, Peter hopped over where he could get a good look at the stranger. The sun was shining full on him, and he wasn't black at all. Jenny Wren was right. For the most part he was very dark green. At least, that is what Peter thought at first glance. Then, as the stranger moved, he seemed to be a rich purple in places. In short he changed color as he turned. His feathers were like those of Creaker the Grackle—iridescent. All over he was speckled with tiny light spots. Underneath he was dark brownish-gray. His wings and tail were of the same color, with little touches of buff. His rather large bill was yellow.

Peter hurried back to Jenny Wren and it must be confessed he looked sheepish. "You were right, Jenny Wren; he isn't black at all," confessed Peter. "Of course I was right. I usually am," retorted Jenny. "He isn't black, he isn't even related to the Blackbird family, and he hasn't any business in the Old Orchard. In fact, if you ask me, he hasn't any business in this country anyway. He's a foreigner. That's what he is—a foreigner."

"But you haven't told me who he is," protested Peter.

"He is Speckles the Starling, and he isn't really an American at all," replied Jenny. "He comes from across the ocean the same as Bully the English Sparrow. Thank goodness he hasn't such a quarrelsome disposition as Bully. Just the same, the rest of us would be better satisfied if he were not here. He has taken possession of one of the old homes of Yellow Wing the Flicker, and that means one less house for birds who really belong here. If his family increases at the rate Bully's family does, I'm afraid some of us will soon be crowded out of the Old Orchard. Did you notice that yellow bill of his?"

Peter nodded. "I certainly did," said he. "I couldn't very well help noticing it."

"Well, there's a funny thing about that bill," replied Jenny. "In winter it turns almost black. Most of us wear a different colored suit in winter, but our bills remain the same."

"Well, he seems to be pretty well fixed here, and I don't see but what the thing for the rest of you birds to do is to make the best of the matter," said Peter. "What I want to know is whether or not he is of any use."

"I guess he must do some good," admitted Jenny Wren rather grudgingly. "I've seen him picking up worms and grubs, but he likes grain, and I have a suspicion that if his family becomes very numerous, and I suspect it will, they will eat more of Farmer Brown's grain than they will pay for by the worms and bugs they destroy. Hello! There's Dandy the Waxwing and his friends."

A flock of modestly dressed yet rather distinguished looking feathered folks had alighted in a cherry-tree and promptly began to help themselves to Farmer Brown's cherries. They were about the size of Winsome Bluebird, but did not look in the least like him, for they were dressed almost wholly in beautiful, rich, soft grayish-brown. Across the end of each tail was a yellow band. On each, the forehead, chin and a line through each eye was velvety-black. Each wore a very stylish pointed cap, and on the wings of most of them were little spots of red which looked like sealing-wax, and from which they get the name of Waxwings. They were slim and trim and quite dandified, and in a quiet way were really beautiful.

As Peter watched them he began to wonder if Farmer Brown would have any cherries left. Peter himself can do pretty well in the matter of stuffing his stomach, but even he marvelled at the way those birds put the cherries out of sight. It was quite clear to him why they are often called Cherrybirds.

"If they stay long, Farmer Brown won't have any cherries left," remarked Peter.

"Don't worry," replied Jenny Wren. "They won't stay long. I don't know anybody equal to them for roaming about. Here are most of us with families on our hands and Mr. and Mrs. Bluebird with a second family and Mr. and Mrs. Robin with a second set of eggs, while those gadabouts up there haven't even begun to think about housekeeping yet. They certainly do like those cherries, but I guess Farmer Brown can stand the loss of what they eat. He may have fewer cherries, but he'll have more apples because of them."

"How's that?" demanded Peter.

"Oh," replied Jenny Wren, "they were over here a while ago

when those little green cankerworms threatened to eat up the whole orchard, and they stuffed themselves on those worms just the same as they are stuffing themselves on cherries now. They are very fond of small fruits but most of those they eat are the wild kind which are of no use at all to Farmer Brown or anybody else. Now just look at that performance, will you?"

There were five of the Waxwings and they were now seated side by side on a branch of the cherry tree. One of them had a plump cherry which he passed to the next one. This one passed it on to the next, and so it went to the end of the row and halfway back before it was finally eaten. Peter laughed right out. "Never in my life have I seen such politeness," said he.

"Huh!" exclaimed Jenny Wren. "I don't believe it was politeness at all. I guess if you got at the truth of the matter you would find that each one was stuffed so full that he thought he didn't have room for that cherry and so passed it along."

"Well, I think that was politeness just the same," retorted Peter. "The first one might have dropped the cherry if he couldn't eat it instead of passing it along." Just then the Waxwings flew away.

It was the very middle of the summer before Peter Rabbit again saw Dandy the Waxwing. Quite by chance he discovered Dandy sitting on the tiptop of an evergreen tree, as if on guard. He was on guard, for in that tree was his nest, though Peter didn't know it at the time. In fact, it was so late in the summer that most of Peter's friends were through nesting and he had quite lost interest in nests. Presently Dandy flew down to a lower branch and there he was joined by Mrs. Waxwing. Then Peter was treated to one of the prettiest sights he ever had seen. They rubbed their bills together as if kissing. They smoothed each other's feathers and altogether were a perfect picture of two little lovebirds. Peter couldn't think of another couple who appeared quite so gentle and loving.

Late in the fall Peter saw Mr. and Mrs. Waxwing and their family together. They were in a cedar tree and were picking off and eating the cedar berries as busily as the five Waxwings had picked Farmer Brown's cherries in the early summer. Peter didn't know it but because of their fondness for cedar berries the Waxwings were often called Cedarbirds or Cedar Waxwings.

XXXVII. Farewells and Welcomes.

All through the long summer Peter Rabbit watched his feathered friends and learned things in regard to their ways he never had suspected. As he saw them keeping the trees of the Old Orchard free of insect pests working in Farmer Brown's garden, and picking up the countless seeds of weeds everywhere, he began to understand something of the wonderful part these feathered folks have in keeping the Great World beautiful and worth while living in.

He had many a hearty laugh as he watched the bird babies learn to fly and to find their own food. All summer long they were going to school all about him, learning how to watch out for danger, to use their eyes and ears, and all the things a bird must know who would live to grow up.

As autumn drew near Peter discovered that his friends were gathering in flocks, roaming here and there. It was one of the first signs that summer was nearly over, and it gave him just a little feeling of sadness. He heard few songs now, for the singing season was over. Also he discovered that many of the most beautifully dressed of his feathered friends had changed their finery for sober traveling suits in preparation for the long journey to the far South where they would spend the winter. In fact he actually failed to recognize some of them at first.

September came, and as the days grew shorter, some of Peter's friends bade him good-by. They were starting on the long journey, planning to take it in easy stages for the most part. Each day saw some slip away. As Peter thought of the dangers of the long trip before them he wondered if he would ever see them again. But some there were who lingered even after Jack Frost's first visit. Welcome and Mrs. Robin, Winsome and Mrs. Bluebird. Little Friend the Song Sparrow and his wife were among these. By and by even they were forced to leave.

Sad indeed and lonely would these days have been for Peter had it not been that with the departure of the friends he had spent so many happy hours with came the arrival of certain other friends from the Far North where they had made their summer homes. Some of these stopped for a few days in passing. Others came to stay, and Peter was kept busy looking for and welcoming them.

A few old friends there were who would stay the year through. Sammy Jay was one. Downy and Hairy the Woodpeckers were others. And one there was whom Peter loves dearly. It was Tommy Tit the Chickadee.

Now Tommy Tit had not gone north in the spring. In fact, he had made his home not very far from the Old Orchard. It just happened that Peter hadn't found that home, and had caught only one or two glimpses of Tommy Tit. Now, with household cares ended and his good-sized family properly started in life, Tommy Tit was no longer interested in the snug little home he had built in a hollow birch-stub, and he and Mrs. Chickadee spent their time flitting about hither, thither, and yon, spreading good cheer. Every time Peter visited the Old Orchard he found him there, and as Tommy was always ready for a bit of merry gossip, Peter soon ceased to miss Jenny Wren.

"Don't you dread the winter, Tommy Tit?" asked Peter one day, as he watched Tommy clinging head down to a twig as he picked some tiny insect eggs from the under side.

"Not a bit," replied Tommy. "I like winter. I like cold weather. It makes a fellow feel good from the tips of his claws to the tip of his bill. I'm thankful I don't have to take that long journey most of the birds have to. I discovered a secret a long time ago, Peter; shall I tell it to you?"

"Please, Tommy," cried Peter. "You know how I love secrets."

"Well," replied Tommy Tit, "this is it: If a fellow keeps his stomach filled he will keep his toes warm."

Peter looked a little puzzled. "I—I—don't just see what your stomach has to do with your toes," said he.

Tommy Tit chuckled. It was a lovely throaty little chuckle. "Dee, dee, dee!" said he. "What I mean is, if a fellow has plenty to eat he will keep the cold out, and I've found that if a fellow uses his eyes and isn't afraid of a little work, he can find plenty to eat. At least I can. The only time I ever get really worried is when the trees are covered with ice. If it were not that Farmer Brown's boy is thoughtful enough to hang a piece of suet in a tree for me, I should dread those ice storms more than I do. As I said before, plenty of food keeps a fellow warm."

"I thought it was your coat of feathers that kept you warm," said Peter.

"Oh, the feathers help," replied Tommy Tit. "Food makes heat and a warm coat keeps the heat in the body. But the heat has got to be there first, or the feathers will do no good. It's just the same way with your own self, Peter. You know you are never really warm in winter unless you have plenty to eat..."

"That's so," replied Peter thoughtfully. "I never happened to think of it before. Just the same, I don't see how you find food enough on the trees when they are all bare in winter."

"Dee, Dee, Chickadee!
Leave that matter just to me,"

Chuckled Tommy Tit. "You ought to know by this time Peter Rabbit, that a lot of different kinds of bugs lay eggs on the twigs and trunks of trees. Those eggs would stay there all winter and in the spring hatch out into lice and worms if it were not for me. Why, sometimes in a single day I find and eat almost five hundred eggs of those little green plant lice that do so much damage in the spring and summer. Then there are little worms that bore in just under the bark, and there are other creatures who sleep the winter away in little cracks in the bark. Oh, there is plenty for me to do in the winter. I am one of the policemen of the trees. Downy and Hairy the Woodpeckers, Seep-Seep the Brown Creeper and Yank-Yank the Nuthatch are others. If we didn't stay right here on the job all winter, I don't know what would become of the Old Orchard."

Tommy Tit hung head downward from a twig while he picked

TOMMY TIT THE CHICKADEE, Tommy will introduce himself.
YANK-YANK THE WHITE-BREASTED NUTHATCH. A winter visitor who goes down a tree head first.

some tiny insect eggs from the under side of it. It didn't seem to make the least difference to Tommy whether he was right side up or upside down. He was a little animated bunch of black and white feathers, not much bigger than Jenny Wren. The top of his head, back of his neck and coat were shining black. The sides of his head and neck were white. His back was ashy. His sides were a soft cream-buff, and his wing and tail feathers were edged with white. His tiny bill was black, and his little black eyes snapped and twinkled in a way good to see. Not one among all Peter's friends is such a merry-hearted little fellow as Tommy Tit the Chickadee. Merriment and happiness bubble out of him all the time, no matter what the weather is. He is the friend of everyone and seems to feel that everyone is his friend.

"I've noticed," said Peter, "that birds who do not sing at any other time of year sing in the spring. Do you have a spring song, Tommy Tit?"

"Well, I don't know as you would call it a song, Peter," chuckled Tommy. "No, I hardly think you would call it a song. But I have a little love call then which goes like this: Phoe-be! Phoe-be!"

It was the softest, sweetest little whistle, and Tommy had rightly called it a love call. "Why, I've often heard that in the spring and didn't know it was your voice at all," cried Peter. "You say Phoebe plainer than does the bird who is named Phoebe, and it is ever so much softer and sweeter. I guess that is because you whistle it."

"I guess you guess right," replied Tommy Tit. "Now I can't stop to talk any longer. These trees need my attention. I want Farmer Brown's boy to feel that I have earned that suet I am sure he will put out for me as soon as the snow and ice come. I'm not the least bit afraid of Farmer Brown's boy. I had just as soon take food from his hand as from anywhere else. He knows I like chopped-up nut-meats, and last winter I used to feed from his hand every day." Peter's eyes opened very wide with surprise. "Do you mean to say," said he, "that you and Farmer Brown's boy are such friends that you dare sit on his hand?"

Tommy Tit nodded his little black-capped head vigorously. "Certainly," said he. "Why not? What's the good of having friends if you can't trust them? The more you trust them the better friends they'll be."

"Just the same, I don't see how you dare to do it," Peter replied. "I know Farmer Brown's boy is the friend of all the little people, and I'm not much afraid of him myself, but just the same I wouldn't dare go near enough for him to touch me."

"Pooh!" retorted Tommy Tit. "That's no way of showing true friendship. You've no idea, Peter, what a comfortable feeling it is to know that you can trust a friend, and I feel that Farmer Brown's boy is one of the best friends I've got. I wish more boys and girls were like him."

XXXVIII. Honker and Dippy Arrive.

The leaves of the trees turned yellow and red and brown and then began to drop, a few at first, then more and more every day until all but the spruce-trees and the pine-trees and the hemlock-trees and the fir-trees and the cedar-trees were bare. By this time most of Peter's feathered friends of the summer had departed, and there were days when Peter had oh, such a lonely feeling. The fur of his coat was growing thicker. The grass of the Green Meadows had turned brown. All these things were signs which Peter knew well. He knew that rough Brother North Wind and Jack Frost were on their way down from the Far North.

Peter had few friends to visit now. Johnny Chuck had gone to sleep for the winter 'way down in his little bedroom under ground. Grandfather Frog had also gone to sleep. So had Old Mr. Toad. Peter spent a great deal of time in the dear Old Briar-patch just sitting still and listening. What he was listening for he didn't know. It just seemed to him that there was something he ought to hear at this time of year, and so he sat listening and listening and wondering what he was listening for. Then, late one afternoon, there came floating down to him from high up in the sky, faintly at first but growing louder, a sound unlike any Peter had heard all the long summer through. The sound was a voice. Rather it was many voices mingled "Honk, honk, honk, honk, honk, honk, honk!" Peter gave a little jump.

"That's what I've been listening for!" he cried. "Honker the Goose and his friends are coming. Oh, I do hope they will stop where I can pay them a call."

He hopped out to the edge of the dear Old Briar-patch that

he might see better, and looked up in the sky. High up, flying in the shape of a letter V, he saw a flock of great birds flying steadily from the direction of the Far North. By the sound of their voices he knew that they had flown far that day and were tired. One bird was in the lead and this he knew to be his old friend, Honker. Straight over his head they passed and as Peter listened to their voices he felt within him the very spirit of the Far North, that great, wild, lonely land which he had never seen but of which he had so often heard.

As Peter watched, Honker suddenly turned and headed in the direction of the Big River. Then he began to slant down, his flock following him. And presently they disappeared behind the trees along the bank of the Great River. Peter gave a happy little sigh. "They are going to spend the night there," thought he. "When the moon comes up, I will run over there, for they will come ashore and I know just where. Now that they have arrived I know that winter is not far away. Honker's voice is as sure a sign of the coming of winter as is Winsome Bluebird's that spring will soon be here."

Peter could hardly wait for the coming of the Black Shadows, and just as soon as they had crept out over the Green Meadows he started for the Big River. He knew just where to go, because he knew that Honker and his friends would rest and spend the night in the same place they had stopped at the year before. He knew that they would remain out in the middle of the Big River until the Black Shadows had made it quite safe for them to swim in. He reached the bank of the Big River just as sweet Mistress Moon was beginning to throw her silvery light over the Great World. There was a sandy bar in the Great River at this point, and Peter squatted on the bank just where this sandy bar began.

It seemed to Peter that he had sat there half the night, but really it was only a short time, before he heard a low signal out in the Black Shadows which covered the middle of the Big River. It was the voice of Honker. Then Peter saw little silvery lines moving on the water and presently a dozen great shapes appeared in the moonlight. Honker and his friends were swimming in. The long neck of each of those great birds was stretched to its full height, and Peter knew that each bird was listening for the slightest suspicious sound. Slowly they drew near, Honker in the lead. They were a picture of perfect caution. When they reached the sandy bar they remained quiet, looking and listening for some time. Then, sure that all was safe, Honker gave a low signal and at once a low gabbling began as the big birds relaxed their watchfulness and came out on the sandy bar, all save one. That one was the guard, and he remained with neck erect on watch. Some swam in among the rushes growing in the water very near to where Peter was sitting and began to feed. Others sat on the sandy bar and dressed their feathers. Honker himself came ashore close to where Peter was sitting.

"Oh, Honker," cried Peter, "I'm so glad you're back here safe and sound."

Honker gave a little start, but instantly recognizing Peter, came over close to him. As he stood there in the moonlight he was truly handsome. His throat and a large patch on each side of his head were white. The rest of his head and long, slim neck were black. His short tail was also black. His back, wings, breast and sides were a soft grayish-brown. He was white around the base of his tail and he wore a white collar.

"Hello, Peter," said he. "It is good to have an old friend greet me. I certainly am glad to be back safe and sound, for the hunters with terrible guns have been at almost every one of our resting places, and it has been hard work to get enough to eat. It is a relief to find one place where there are no terrible guns."

"Have you come far?" asked Peter.

"Very far, Peter; very far," replied Honker. "And we still have very far to go. I shall be thankful when the journey is over, for on me depends the safety of all those with me, and it is a great responsibility."

"Will winter soon be here?" asked Peter eagerly.

"Rough Brother North Wind and Jack Frost were right behind us," replied Honker. "You know we stay in the Far North just as long as we can. Already the place where we nested is frozen and covered with snow. For the first part of the journey we kept only just ahead of the snow and ice, but as we drew near to where men make their homes we were forced to make longer journeys each day, for the places where it is safe to feed and rest are few and far between. Now we shall hurry on until we reach the place in the far-away South where we will make our winter home."

Just then Honker was interrupted by wild, strange sounds from the middle of the Great River. It sounded like crazy laughter. Peter jumped at the sound, but Honker merely chuckled. "It's Dippy the Loon," said he. "He spent the summer in the Far North not far from us. He started south just before we did."

"I wish he would come in here so that I can get a good look at him and make his acquaintance," said Peter.

"He may, but I doubt it," replied Honker. "He and his mate are great people to keep by themselves. Then, too, they don't have to come ashore for food. You know Dippy feeds altogether on fish. He really has an easier time on the long journey than we do, because he can get his food without running so much risk of being shot by the terrible hunters. He practically lives on the water. He's about the most awkward fellow on land of any one I know."

"Why should he be any more awkward on land then you?" asked Peter, his curiosity aroused at once.

"Because," replied Honker, "Old Mother Nature has given him very short legs and has placed them so far back on his body that he can't keep his balance to walk, and has to use his wings and bill to help him over the ground. On shore he is about the most helpless thing you can imagine. But on water he is another fellow altogether. He's just as much at home under water as on top. My, how that fellow can dive! When he sees the flash of a gun he will get under water before the shot can reach him. That's where he has the advantage of us Geese. You know we can't dive. He could swim clear across this river under water if he wanted to, and he can go so fast under water that he can catch a fish. It is because his legs have been placed so far back that he can swim so fast. You know his feet are nothing but big paddles. Another funny thing is that he can sink right down in the water when he wants to, with nothing but his head out. I envy him that. It would be a lot easier for us Geese to escape the dreadful hunters if we could sink down that way."

"Has he a bill like yours?" asked Peter innocently.

"Of course not," replied Honker. "Didn't I tell you that he lives on fish? How do you suppose he would hold on to his slippery fish if he had a broad bill like mine? His bill is stout, straight and sharp pointed. He is rather a handsome fellow. He is pretty nearly as big as I am, and his back, wings, tail and neck are black with bluish or greenish appearance in the sun. His back and wings are spotted with white, and there are streaks of white on his throat and the sides of his neck. On his breast and below he is all white. You certainly ought to get acquainted with Dippy, Peter, for there isn't anybody quite like him."

"I'd like to," replied Peter. "But if he never comes to shore, how can I? I guess I will have to be content to know him just by his voice. I certainly never will forget that. It's about as crazy sounding as the voice of Old Man Coyote, and that is saying a great deal."

"There's one thing I forgot to tell you," said Honker. "Dippy can't fly from the land; he must be on the water in order to get up in the air."

"You can, can't you?" asked Peter.

"Of course I can," replied Honker. "Why, we Geese get a lot of our food on land. When it is safe to do so we visit the grain fields and pick up the grain that has been shaken out during harvest. Of course we couldn't do that if we couldn't fly from the land. We can rise from either land or water equally well. Now if you'll excuse me, Peter, I'll take a nap. My, but I'm tired! And I've got a long journey to-morrow."

So Peter politely bade Honker and his relatives good-night and left them in peace on the sandy bar in the Big River.

XXXIX. Peter Discovers Two Old Friends.

Rough Brother North Wind and Jack Frost were not far behind Honker the Goose. In a night Peter Rabbit's world was transformed. It had become a new world, a world of pure white. The last laggard among Peter's feathered friends who spend the winter in the far-away South had hurried away. Still Peter was not lonely. Tommy Tit's cheery voice greeted Peter the very first thing that morning after the storm. Tommy seemed to be in just as good spirits as ever he had been in summer.

Now Peter rather likes the snow. He likes to run about in it, and so he followed Tommy Tit up to the Old Orchard. He felt sure that he would find company there besides Tommy Tit, and he was not disappointed. Downy and Hairy the Woodpeckers were getting their breakfast from a piece of suet Farmer Brown's boy had thoughtfully fastened in one of the apple-trees for them. Sammy Jay was there also, and his blue coat never had looked better than it did against the pure white of the snow.

These were the only ones Peter really had expected to find in the Old Orchard, and so you can guess how pleased he was as he hopped over the old stone wall to hear the voice of one whom he had almost forgotten. It was the voice of Yank-Yank the Nuthatch, and while it was far from being sweet there was in it something of good cheer and contentment. At once Peter hurried in the direction from which it came.

On the trunk of an apple-tree he caught sight of a gray and black and white bird about the size of Downy the Woodpecker. The top of his head and upper part of his back were shining black. The rest of his back was bluish-gray. The sides of his head and his breast were white. The outer feathers of his tail were black with white patches near their tips.

But Peter didn't need to see how Yank-Yank was dressed in order to recognize him. Peter would have known him if he had been so far away that the colors of his coat did not show at all. You see, Yank-Yank was doing a most surprising thing, something no other bird can do. He was walking head first down the trunk of that tree, picking tiny eggs of insects from the bark and seemingly quite as much at home and quite as unconcerned in that queer position as if he were right side up.

As Peter approached, Yank-Yank lifted his head and called a greeting which sounded very much like the repetition of his own name. Then he turned around and began to climb the tree as easily as he had come down it.

"Welcome home, Yank-Yank!" cried Peter, hurrying up quite out of breath.

Yank-Yank turned around so that he was once more head down, and his eyes twinkled as he looked down at Peter. "You're mistaken Peter," said he. "This isn't home. I've simply come down here for the winter. You know home is where you raise your children, and my home is in the Great Woods farther north. There is too much ice and snow up there, so I have come down here to spend the winter."

"Well anyway, it's a kind of home; it's your winter home," protested Peter, "and I certainly am glad to see you back. The Old Orchard wouldn't be quite the same without you. Did you have a pleasant summer? And if you please, Yank-Yank, tell me where you built your home and what it was like."

"Yes, Mr. Curiosity, I had a very pleasant summer," replied Yank-Yank. "Mrs. Yank-Yank and I raised a family of six and that is doing a lot better than some folks I know, if I do say it. As to our nest, it was made of leaves and feathers and it was in a hole in a certain old stump that not a soul knows of but Mrs. Yank-Yank and myself. Now is there anything else you want to know?"

"Yes," retorted Peter promptly. "I want to know how it is that you can walk head first down the trunk of a tree without losing your balance and tumbling off."

Yank-Yank chuckled happily. "I discovered a long time ago,

Peter," said he, "that the people who get on best in this world are those who make the most of what they have and waste no time wishing they could have what other people have. I suppose you have noticed that all the Woodpecker family have stiff tail feathers and use them to brace themselves when they are climbing a tree. They have become so dependent on them that they don't dare move about on the trunk of a tree without using them. If they want to come down a tree they have to back down.

"Now Old Mother Nature didn't give me stiff tail feathers, but she gave me a very good pair of feet with three toes in front and one behind and when I was a very little fellow I learned to make the most of those feet. Each toe has a sharp claw. When I go up a tree the three front claws on each foot hook into the bark. When I come down a tree I simply twist one foot around so that I can use the claws of this foot to keep me from falling. It is just as easy for me to go down a tree as it is to go up, and I can go right around the trunk just as easily and comfortably." Suiting action to the word, Yank-Yank ran around the trunk of the apple-tree just above Peter's head. When he reappeared Peter had another question ready.

"Do you live altogether on grubs and worms and insects and their eggs?" he asked.

"I should say not!" exclaimed Yank-Yank. "I like acorns and beechnuts and certain kinds of seeds."

"I don't see how such a little fellow as you can eat such hard things as acorns and beechnuts," protested Peter a little doubtfully.

Yank-Yank laughed right out. "Sometime when I see you over in the Green Forest I'll show you," said he. "When I find a fat beechnut I take it to a little crack in a tree that will just hold it; then with this stout bill of mine I crack the shell. It really is quite easy when you know how. Cracking a nut open that way is sometimes called hatching, and that is how I come by the name of Nuthatch. Hello! There's Seep-Seep. I haven't seen him since we were together up North. His home was not far from mine."

As Yank-Yank spoke, a little brown bird alighted at the very foot of the next tree. He was just a trifle bigger than Jenny Wren but not at all like Jenny, for while Jenny's tail usually is cocked up in the sauciest way, Seep-Seep's tail is never cocked up at all. In fact, it bends down, for Seep-Seep uses his tail just as the members of the Woodpecker family use theirs. He was dressed in grayish-brown above and grayish-white beneath. Across each wing was a little band of buffy-white, and his bill was curved just a little.

Seep-Seep didn't stop an instant but started up the trunk of that tree, going round and round it as he climbed, and picking out things to eat from under the bark. His way of climbing that tree was very like creeping, and Peter thought to himself that Seep-Seep was well named the Brown Creeper. He knew it was quite useless to try to get Seep-Seep to talk, He knew that Seep-Seep wouldn't waste any time that way.

Round and round up the trunk of the tree he went, and when he reached the top at once flew down to the bottom of the next tree and without a pause started up that. He wasted no time exploring the branches, but stuck to the trunk. Once in a while he would cry in a thin little voice, "Seep! Seep!" but never paused to rest or look around. If he had felt that on him alone depended the job of getting all the insect eggs and grubs on those trees he could not have been more industrious.

"Does he build his nest in a hole in a tree?" asked Peter of Yank-Yank. Yank-Yank shook his head. "No," he replied. "He hunts for a tree or stub with a piece of loose bark hanging to it. In behind this he tucks his nest made of twigs, strips of bark and moss. He's a funny little fellow and I don't know of any one in all the great world who more strictly attends to his own business than does Seep-Seep the Brown Creeper. By the way, Peter, have you seen anything of Dotty the Tree Sparrow?"

"Not yet," replied Peter, "but I think he must be here. I'm glad you reminded me of him. I'll go look for him."

XL. Some Merry Seed-Eaters.

Having been reminded of Dotty the Tree Sparrow, Peter Rabbit became possessed of a great desire to find this little friend of the cold months and learn how he had fared through the summer.

He was at a loss just where to look for Dotty until he remembered a certain weedy field along the edge of which the bushes had been left growing. "Perhaps I'll find him there," thought Peter, for he remembered that Dotty lives almost wholly on seeds, chiefly weed seeds, and that he dearly loves a weedy field with bushes not far distant in which he can hide.

So Peter hurried over to the weedy field and there, sure enough, he found Dotty with a lot of his friends. They were very busy getting their breakfast. Some were clinging to the weed-stalks picking the seeds out of the tops, while others were picking up the seeds from the ground. It was cold. Rough Brother North Wind was doing his best to blow up another snow-cloud. It wasn't at all the kind of day in which one would expect to find anybody in high spirits. But Dotty was. He was even singing as Peter came up, and all about Dotty's friends and relatives were twittering as happily and merrily as if it were the beginning of spring instead of winter.

Dotty was very nearly the size of Little Friend the Song Sparrow and looked somewhat like him, save that his breast was clear ashy-gray, all but a little dark spot in the middle, the little dot from which he gets his name. He wore a chestnut cap, almost exactly like that of Chippy the Chipping Sparrow. It reminded Peter that Dotty is often called the Winter Chippy.

"Welcome back, Dotty!" cried Peter. "It does my heart good

to see you."

"Thank you, Peter," twittered Dotty happily. "In a way it is good to be back. Certainly, it is good to know that an old friend is glad to see me."

"Are you going to stay all winter, Dotty?" asked Peter.

"I hope so," replied Dotty. "I certainly shall if the snow does not get so deep that I cannot get enough to eat. Some of these weeds are so tall that it will take a lot of snow to cover them, and as long as the tops are above the snow I will have nothing to worry about. You know a lot of seeds remain in these tops all winter. But if the snow gets deep enough to cover these I shall have to move along farther south."

"Then I hope there won't be much snow," declared Peter very emphatically. "There are few enough folks about in winter at best, goodness knows, and I don't know of any one I enjoy having for a neighbor more than I do you."

"Thank you again, Peter," cried Dotty, "and please let me return the compliment. I like cold weather. I like winter when there isn't too much ice and bad weather. I always feel good in cold weather. That is one reason I go north to nest."

"Speaking of nests, do you build in a tree?" inquired Peter.

"Usually on or near the ground," replied Dotty. "You know I am really a ground bird although I am called a Tree Sparrow. Most of us Sparrows spend our time on or near the ground."

"I know," replied Peter. "Do you know I'm very fond of the Sparrow family. I just love your cousin Chippy, who nests in the Old Orchard every spring. I wish he would stay all winter. I really don't see why he doesn't. I should think he could if you can."

Dotty laughed. It was a tinkling little laugh, good to hear. "Cousin Chippy would starve to death," he declared. "It is all a matter of food. You ought to know that by this time, Peter. Cousin Chippy lives chiefly on worms and bugs and I live almost wholly on seeds, and that is what makes the difference. Cousin Chippy must go where he can get plenty to eat. I can get plenty here and so I stay."

"Did you and your relatives come down from the Far North alone?" asked Peter.

"No," replied Dotty promptly. "Slaty the Junco and his rela-

SNOWFLAKE THE SNOW BUNTING, the one small bird who is largely white. WANDERER THE HORNED LARK. His yellow throat and forehead and the two little tufts of feathers, like tiny horns, will always identify him.

tives came along with us and we had a very merry party."

Peter pricked up his ears. "Is Slaty here now?" he asked eagerly.

"Very much here," replied a voice right behind Peter's back. It was so unexpected that it made Peter jump. He turned to find Slaty himself chuckling merrily as he picked up seeds. He was very nearly the same size as Dotty but trimmer. In fact he was one of the trimmest, neatest appearing of all of Peter's friends. There was no mistaking Slaty the Junco for any other bird. His head, throat and breast were clear slate color. Underneath he was white. His sides were grayish. His outer tail feathers were white. His bill was flesh color. It looked almost white.

"Welcome! Welcome!" cried Peter. "Are you here to stay all winter?"

"I certainly am," was Slaty's prompt response. "It will take pretty bad weather to drive me away from here. If the snow gets too deep I'll just go up to Farmer Brown's barnyard. I can always pick up a meal there, for Farmer Brown's boy is a very good friend of mine. I know he won't let me starve, no matter what the weather is. I think it is going to snow some more. I like the snow. You know I am sometimes called the Snowbird."

Peter nodded. "So I have heard," said he, "though I think that name really belongs to Snowflake the Snow Bunting."

"Quite right, Peter, quite right," replied Slaty. "I much prefer my own name of Junco. My, these seeds are good!" All the time he was busily picking up seeds so tiny that Peter didn't even see them.

"If you like here so much why don't you stay all the year?" inquired Peter.

"It gets too warm," replied Slaty promptly,

"I hate hot weather. Give me cold weather every time."

"Do you mean to tell me that it is cold all summer where you nest in the Far North?" demanded Peter.

"Not exactly cold," replied Slaty, "but a lot cooler than it is down here. I don't go as far north to nest as Snowflake does, but I go far enough to be fairly comfortable. I don't see how some folks can stand hot weather."

"It is a good thing they can," interrupted Dotty. "If everybody liked the same things it wouldn't do at all. Just suppose all the birds ate nothing but seeds. There wouldn't be seeds enough to go around, and a lot of us would starve. Then, too, the worms and the bugs would eat up everything. So, take it all together, it is a mighty good thing that some birds live almost wholly on worms and bugs and such things, leaving the seeds to the rest of us. I guess Old Mother Nature knew what she was about when she gave us different tastes."

Peter nodded his head in approval. "You can always trust Old Mother Nature to know what is best," said he sagely. "By the way, Slaty, what do you make your nest of and where do you put it?"

"My nest is usually made of grasses, moss and rootlets. Sometimes it is lined with fine grasses, and when I am lucky enough to find them I use long hairs. Often I put my nest on the ground, and never very far above it. I am like my friend Dotty in this respect. It always seems to me easier to hide a nest on the ground than anywhere else. There is nothing like having a nest well hidden. It takes sharp eyes to find my nest, I can tell you that, Peter Rabbit."

Just then Dotty, who had been picking seeds out of the top of a weed, gave a cry of alarm and instantly there was a flit of many wings as Dotty and his relatives and Slaty sought the shelter of the bushes along the edge of the field. Peter sat up very straight and looked this way and looked that way. At first he saw nothing suspicious. Then, crouching flat among the weeds, he got a glimpse of Black Pussy, the cat from Farmer Brown's house. She had been creeping up in the hope of catching one of those happy little seedeaters. Peter stamped angrily. Then with long jumps he started for the dear Old Briar-patch, lipperty-lipperty-lip, for truth to tell, big as he was, he was a little afraid of Black Pussy.

XLI. More Friends Come With the Snow.

Slaty the Junco had been quite right in thinking it was going to snow some more. Rough Brother North Wind hurried up one big cloud after another, and late that afternoon the white feathery flakes came drifting down out of the sky.

Peter Rabbit sat tight in the dear Old Briar-patch. In fact Peter did no moving about that night, but remained squatting just inside the entrance to an old hole Johnny Chuck's grandfather had dug long ago in the middle of the dear Old Briar-patch. Some time before morning the snow stopped falling and then rough Brother North Wind worked as hard to blow away the clouds as he had done to bring them.

When jolly, round, bright Mr. Sun began his daily climb up in the blue, blue sky he looked down on a world of white. It seemed as if every little snowflake twinkled back at every little sunbeam. It was all very lovely, and Peter Rabbit rejoiced as he scampered forth in quest of his breakfast.

He started first for the weedy field where the day before he had found Dotty the Tree Sparrow and Slaty the Junco. They were there before him, having the very best time ever was as they picked seeds from the tops of the weeds which showed above the snow. Almost at once Peter discovered that they were not the only seekers for seeds. Walking about on the snow, and quite as busy seeking seeds as were Dotty and Slaty, was a bird very near their size the top of whose head, neck and back were a soft rusty-brown. There was some black on his wings, but the latter were mostly white and the outer tail feathers were white. His breast and under parts were white. It was Snowflake the Snow Bunting in his winter suit. Peter knew him instantly.

There was no mistaking him, for, as Peter well knew, there is no other bird of his size and shape who is so largely white. He had appeared so unexpectedly that it almost seemed as if he must have come out of the snow clouds just as had the snow itself. Peter had his usual question ready.

"Are you going to spend the winter here, Snowflake?" he cried.

Snowflake was so busy getting his breakfast that he did not reply at once. Peter noticed that he did not hop, but walked or ran. Presently he paused long enough to reply to Peter's question. "If the snow has come to stay all winter, perhaps I'll stay," said he.

"What has the snow to do with it?" demanded Peter.

"Only that I like the snow and I like cold weather. When the snow begins to disappear, I just naturally fly back farther north," replied Snowflake. "It isn't that I don't like bare ground, because I do, and I'm always glad when the snow is blown off in places so that I can hunt for seeds on the ground. But when the snow begins to melt everywhere I feel uneasy. I can't understand how folks can be contented where there is no snow and ice. You don't catch me going 'way down south. No, siree, you don't catch me going 'way down south. Why, when the nesting season comes around, I chase Jack Frost clear 'way up to where he spends the summer. I nest 'way up on the shore of the Polar Sea, but of course you don't know where that is, Peter Rabbit."

"If you are so fond of the cold in the Far North, the snow and the ice, what did you come south at all for? Why don't you stay up there all the year around?" demanded Peter.

"Because, Peter," replied Snowflake, twittering merrily, "like everybody else, I have to eat in order to live. When you see me down here you may know that the snows up north are so deep that they have covered all the seeds. I always keep a weather eye out, as the saying is, and the minute it looks as if there would be too much snow for me to get a living, I move along. I hope I will not have to go any farther than this, but if some morning you wake up and find the snow so deep that all the heads of the weeds are buried, don't expect to find me."

"That's what I call good, sound common sense," said another voice, and a bird a little bigger than Snowflake, and who at first glance seemed to be dressed almost wholly in soft chocolate brown, alighted in the snow close by and at once began to run about in search of seeds. It was Wanderer the Horned Lark. Peter hailed him joyously, for there was something of mystery about Wanderer, and Peter, as you know, loves mystery.

Peter had known him ever since his first winter, yet did not feel really acquainted, for Wanderer seldom stayed long enough for a real acquaintance. Every winter he would come, sometimes two or three times, but seldom staying more than a few days at a time. Quite often he and his relatives appeared with the Snowflakes, for they are the best of friends and travel much together.

Now as Wanderer reached up to pick seeds from a weed-top, Peter had a good look at him. The first things he noticed were the two little horn-like tufts of black feathers above and behind the eyes. It is from these that Wanderer gets the name of Horned Lark. No other bird has anything quite like them. His forehead, a line over each eye, and his throat were yellow. There was a black mark from each corner of the bill curving downward just below the eye and almost joining a black crescent-shaped band across the breast. Beneath this he was soiled white with dusky spots showing here and there. His back was brown, in places having almost a pinkish tinge. His tail was black, showing a little white on the edges when he flew. All together he was a handsome little fellow.

"Do all of your family have those funny little horns?" asked Peter.

"No," was Wanderer's prompt reply. "Mrs. Lark does not have them."

"I think they are very becoming," said Peter politely.

"Thank you," replied Wanderer. "I am inclined to agree with you. You should see me when I have my summer suit."

"Is it so very different from this?" asked Peter. "I think your present suit is pretty enough."

"Well said, Peter, well said," interrupted Snowflake. "I quite agree with you. I think Wanderer's present suit is pretty enough for any one, but it is true that his summer suit is even prettier. It isn't so very different, but it is brighter, and those black markings are much stronger and show up better. You see, Wanderer is one of my neighbors in the Far North, and I know all about him."

"And that means that you don't know anything bad about me, doesn't it?" chuckled Wanderer.

Snowflake nodded. "Not a thing," he replied. "I wouldn't ask for a better neighbor. You should hear him sing, Peter. He sings up in the air, and it really is a very pretty song."

"I'd just love to hear him," replied Peter. "Why don't you sing here, Wanderer?"

"This isn't the singing season," replied Wanderer promptly. "Besides, there isn't time to sing when one has to keep busy every minute in order to get enough to eat."

"I don't see," said Peter, "why, when you get here, you don't stay in one place."

"Because it is easier to get a good living by moving about," replied Wanderer promptly. "Besides, I like to visit new places. I shouldn't enjoy being tied down in just one place like some birds I know. Would you, Snowflake?"

Snowflake promptly replied that he wouldn't. Just then Peter discovered something that he hadn't known before. "My goodness," he exclaimed, "what a long claw you have on each hind toe!"

It was true. Each hind claw was about twice as long as any other claw. Peter couldn't see any special use for it and he was just about to ask more about it when Wanderer suddenly spied a flock of his relatives some distance away and flew to join them. Probably this saved him some embarrassment, for it is doubtful if he himself knew why Old Mother Nature had given him such long hind claws.

XLII. PETER LEARNS SOMETHING ABOUT SPOOKY.

PETER RABBIT likes winter. At least he doesn't mind it so very much, even though he has to really work for a living. Perhaps it is a good thing that he does, for he might grow too fat to keep out of the way of Reddy Fox. You see when the snow is deep Peter is forced to eat whatever he can, and very often there isn't much of anything for him but the bark of young trees. It is at such times that Peter gets into mischief, for there is no bark he likes better than that of young fruit trees. Now you know what happens when the bark is taken off all the way around the trunk of a tree. That tree dies. It dies for the simple reason that it is up the inner layer of bark that the life-giving sap travels in the spring and summer. Of course, when a strip of bark has been taken off all the way around near the base of a tree, the sap cannot go up and the tree must die.

Now up near the Old Orchard Farmer Brown had set out a young orchard. Peter knew all about that young orchard, for he had visited it many times in the summer. Then there had been plenty of sweet clover and other green things to eat, and Peter had never been so much as tempted to sample the bark of those young trees. But now things were very different, and it was very seldom that Peter knew what it was to have a full stomach. He kept thinking of that young orchard. He knew that if he were wise he would keep away from there. But the more he thought of it the more it seemed to him that he just must have some of that tender young bark. So just at dusk one evening, Peter started for the young orchard.

Peter got there in safety and his eyes sparkled as he hopped over to the nearest young tree. But when he reached it, Peter had a dreadful disappointment. All around the trunk of that young tree was wire netting. Peter couldn't get even a nibble of that bark. He tried the next tree with no better result. Then he hurried on from tree to tree, always with the same result. You see Farmer Brown knew all about Peter's liking for the bark of young fruit trees, and he had been wise enough to protect his young orchard.

At last Peter gave up and hopped over to the Old Orchard. As he passed a certain big tree he was startled by a voice. "What's the matter, Peter?" said the voice. "You don't look happy."

Peter stopped short and stared up in the big apple-tree. Look as he would he couldn't see anybody. Of course there wasn't a leaf on that tree, and he could see all through it. Peter blinked and felt foolish. He knew that had there been any one sitting on any one of those branches he couldn't have helped seeing him.

"Don't look so high, Peter; don't look so high," said the voice with a chuckle. This time it sounded as if it came right out of the trunk of the tree. Peter stared at the trunk and then suddenly laughed right out. Just a few feet above the ground was a good sized hole in the tree, and poking his head out of it was a funny little fellow with big eyes and a hooked beak.

"You certainly did fool me that time, Spooky," cried Peter. "I ought to have recognized your voice, but I didn't."

Spooky the Screech Owl, for that is who it was, came out of the hole in the tree and without a sound from his wings flew over and perched just above Peter's head. He was a little fellow, not over eight inches high, but there was no mistaking the family to which he belonged. In fact he looked very much like a small copy of Hooty the Great Horned Owl, so much so that Peter felt a little cold shiver run over him, although he had nothing in the world to fear from Spooky.

His head seemed to be almost as big around as his body, and he seemed to leave no neck at all. He was dressed in bright reddish-brown, with little streaks and bars of black. Underneath he was whitish, with little streaks and bars of black and brown. On each side of his head was a tuft of feathers. They looked like ears and some people think they are ears, which is a mistake. His eyes were round and yellow with a fierce hungry look in them.

SPOOKY THE SCREECH OWL. The most common of all Owls, sometimes reddish-brown and sometimes gray.

His bill was small and almost hidden among the feathers of his face, but it was hooked just like the bill of Hooty. As he settled himself he turned his head around until he could look squarely behind him, then brought it back again so quickly that to Peter it looked as if it had gone clear around. You see Spooky's eyes are fixed in their sockets and he cannot move them from side to side. He has to turn his whole head in order to see to one side or the other.

"You haven't told me yet why you look so unhappy, Peter," said Spooky.

"Isn't an empty stomach enough to make any fellow unhappy?" retorted Peter rather shortly.

Spooky chuckled. "I've got an empty stomach myself, Peter," said he, "but it isn't making me unhappy. I have a feeling that somewhere there is a fat Mouse waiting for me."

Just then Peter remembered what Jenny Wren had told him early in the spring of how Spooky the Screech Owl lives all the year around in a hollow tree, and curiosity made him forget for the time being that he was hungry. "Did you live in that hole all summer, Spooky?" he asked.

Spooky nodded solemnly. "I've lived in that hollow summer and winter for three years," said he.

Peter's eyes opened very wide. "And till now I never even guessed it," he exclaimed. "Did you raise a family there?"

"I certainly did," replied Spooky. "Mrs. Spooky and I raised a family of four as fine looking youngsters as you ever have seen. They've gone out into the Great World to make their own living now. Two were dressed just like me and two were gray."

"What's that?" exclaimed Peter.

"I said that two were dressed just like me and two were gray," replied Spooky rather sharply.

"That's funny," Peter exclaimed.

"What's funny?" snapped Spooky rather crossly.

"Why that all four were not dressed alike," said Peter.

"There's nothing funny about it," retorted Spooky, and snapped his bill sharply with a little cracking sound. "We Screech Owls believe in variety. Some of us are gray and some of us are reddish-brown. It is a case of where you cannot tell a person just by the color of his clothes."

Peter nodded as if he quite understood, although he couldn't understand at all. "I'm ever so pleased to find you living here," said he politely. "You see, in winter the Old Orchard is rather a lonely place. I don't see how you get enough to eat when there are so few birds about."

"Birds!" snapped Spooky. "What have birds to do with it?"

"Why, don't you live on birds?" asked Peter innocently.

"I should say not. I guess I would starve if I depended on birds for my daily food," retorted Spooky. "I catch a Sparrow now and then, to be sure, but usually it is an English Sparrow, and I consider that I am doing the Old Orchard a good turn every time I am lucky enough to catch one of the family of Bully the English Sparrow. But I live mostly on Mice and Shrews in winter and in summer I eat a lot of grasshoppers and other insects. If it wasn't for me and my relatives I guess Mice would soon overrun the Great World. Farmer Brown ought to be glad I've come to live in the Old Orchard and I guess he is, for Farmer Brown's boy knows all about this house of mine and never disturbs me. Now if you'll excuse me I think I'll fly over to Farmer Brown's young orchard. I ought to find a fat Mouse or two trying to get some of the bark from those young trees."

"Huh!" exclaimed Peter. "They can try all they want to, but they won't get any; I can tell you that."

Spooky's round yellow eyes twinkled. "It must be you have been trying to get some of that bark yourself," said he.

Peter didn't say anything but he looked guilty, and Spooky once more chuckled as he spread his wings and flew away so soundlessly that he seemed more like a drifting shadow than a bird. Then Peter started for a certain swamp he knew of where he would be sure to find enough bark to stay his appetite.

XLIII. Queer Feet and a Queerer Bill.

Peter Rabbit had gone over to the Green Forest to call on his cousin, Jumper the Hare, who lives there altogether. He had no difficulty in finding Jumper's tracks in the snow, and by following these he at length came up with Jumper. The fact is, Peter almost bumped into Jumper before he saw him, for Jumper was wearing a coat as white as the snow itself. Squatting under a little snow-covered hemlock-tree he looked like nothing more than a little mound of snow.

"Oh!" cried Peter. "How you startled me! I wish I had a winter coat like yours. It must be a great help in avoiding your enemies."

"It certainly is, Cousin Peter," cried Jumper. "Nine times out of ten all I have to do is to sit perfectly still when there was no wind to carry my scent. I have had Reddy Fox pass within a few feet of me and never suspect that I was near. I hope this snow will last all winter. It is only when there isn't any snow that I am particularly worried. Then I am not easy for a minute, because my white coat can be seen a long distance against the brown of the dead leaves."

Peter chuckled, "that is just when I feel safest," he replied. "I like the snow, but this brown-gray coat of mine certainly does show up against it. Don't you find it pretty lonesome over here in the Green Forest with all the birds gone, Cousin Jumper?"

Jumper shook his head. "Not all have gone, Peter, you know," said he. "Strutter the Grouse and Mrs. Grouse are here, and I see them every day. They've got snowshoes now."

Peter blinked his eyes and looked rather perplexed. "Snowshoes!" he exclaimed. "I don't understand what you mean."

"Come with me," replied Jumper, "and I'll show you."

So Jumper led the way and Peter followed close at his heels. Presently they came to some tracks in the snow. At first glance they reminded Peter of the queer tracks Farmer Brown's ducks made in the mud on the edge of the Smiling Pool in summer. "What funny tracks those are!" he exclaimed. "Who made them?"

"Just keep on following me and you'll see," retorted Jumper.

So they continued to follow the tracks until presently, just ahead of them, they saw Strutter the Grouse. Peter opened his eyes with surprise when he discovered that those queer tracks were made by Strutter.

"Cousin Peter wants to see your snowshoes, Strutter," said Jumper as they came up with him.

Strutter's bright eyes sparkled. "He's just as curious as ever, isn't he?" said he. "Well, I don't mind showing him my snowshoes because I think myself that they are really quite wonderful." He held up one foot with the toes spread apart and Peter saw that growing out from the sides of each toe were queer little horny points set close together. They quite filled the space between his toes. Peter recalled that when he had seen Strutter in the summer those toes had been smooth and that his tracks on soft ground had shown the outline of each toe clearly. "How funny!" exclaimed Peter.

"There's nothing funny about them," retorted Strutter. "If Old Mother Nature hadn't given me something of this kind I certainly would have a hard time of it when there is snow on the ground. If my feet were just the same as in summer I would sink right down in when the snow is soft and wouldn't be able to walk about at all. Now, with these snowshoes I get along very nicely. You see I sink in but very little."

He took three or four steps and Peter saw right away how very useful those snowshoes were. "My!" he exclaimed. "I wish Old Mother Nature would give me snowshoes too." Strutter and Jumper both laughed and after a second Peter laughed with them, for he realized how impossible it would be for him to have anything like those snowshoes of Strutter's.

"Cousin Peter was just saying that he should think I would find it lonesome over here in the Green Forest. He forgot that you and Mrs. Grouse stay all winter, and he forgot that while most of the birds who spent the summer here have left, there are others who come down from the Far North to take their place."

"Who, for instance?" demanded Peter.

"Snipper the Crossbill," replied Jumper promptly. "I haven't seen him yet this winter, but I know he is here because only this morning I found some pine seeds on the snow under a certain tree."

"Huh!" Peter exclaimed. "That doesn't prove anything. Those seeds might have just fallen, or Chatterer the Red Squirrel might have dropped them."

"This isn't the season for seeds to just fall, and I know by the signs that Chatterer hasn't been about," retorted Jumper. "Let's go over there now and see what we will see."

Once more he led the way and Peter followed. As they drew near that certain pine-tree, a short whistled note caused them to look up. Busily at work on a pine cone near the top of a tree was a bird about the size of Bully the English Sparrow. He was dressed wholly in dull red with brownish-black wings and tail.

"What did I tell you?" cried Jumper. "There's Snipper this very minute, and over in that next tree are a lot of his family and relatives. See in what a funny way they climb about among the branches. They don't flit or hop, but just climb around. I don't know of any other bird anywhere around here that does that."

Just then a seed dropped and landed on the snow almost in front of Peter's nose. Almost at once Snipper himself followed it, picking it up and eating it with as much unconcern as if Peter and Jumper were a mile away instead of only a foot or so. The very first thing Peter noticed was Snipper's bill. The upper and lower halves crossed at the tips. That bill looked very much as if Snipper had struck something hard and twisted the tips over.

"Have—have—you met with an accident?" he asked a bit hesitatingly.

Snipper looked surprised. "Are you talking to me?" he asked. "Whatever put such an idea into your head?"

"Your bill," replied Peter promptly. "How did it get twisted like that?"

Snipper laughed. "It isn't twisted," said he. "It is just the way Old Mother Nature made it, and I really don't know what I'd do if it were any different."

Peter scratched one long ear, as is his way when he is puzzled. "I don't see," said he, "how it is possible for you to pick up food with a bill like that."

"And I don't see how I would get my food if I didn't have a bill like this," retorted Snipper. Then, seeing how puzzled Peter really was, he went on to explain. "You see, I live very largely on the seeds that grow in pine cones and the cones of other trees. Of course I eat some other food, such as seeds and buds of trees. But what I love best of all are the seeds that grow in the cones of evergreen trees. If you've ever looked at one of those cones, you will understand that those seeds are not very easy to get at. But with this kind of a bill it is no trouble at all. I can snip them out just as easily as birds with straight bills can pick up seeds. You see my bill is very much like a pair of scissors."

"It really is very wonderful," confessed Peter. "Do you mind telling me, Snipper, why I never have seen you here in summer?"

"For the same reason that in summer you never see Snowflake and Wanderer the Horned Lark and some others I might name," replied Snipper. "Give me the Far North every time. I would stay there the year through but that sometimes food gets scarce up there. That is why I am down here now. If you'll excuse me, I'll go finish my breakfast."

Snipper flew up in the tree where the other Crossbills were at work and Peter and Jumper watched them.

"I suppose you know," said Jumper, "that Snipper has a cousin who looks almost exactly like him with the exception of two white bars on each wing. He is called the White-winged Crossbill."

"I didn't know it," replied Peter, "but I'm glad you've told me. I certainly shall watch out for him. I can't get over those funny bills. No one could ever mistake it for any other bird. Is there anyone else now from the Far North whom I haven't seen?"

XLIV. More Folks in Red.

JUMPER THE Hare didn't have time to reply to Peter Rabbit's question when Peter asked if there was any one else besides the Crossbills who had come down from the Far North.

"I have," said a voice from a tree just back of them.

It was so unexpected that it made both Peter and Jumper hop in startled surprise. Then they turned to see who had spoken. There sat a bird just a little smaller than Welcome Robin, who at first glance seemed to be dressed in strawberry-red. However, a closer look showed that there were slate-gray markings about his head, under his wings and on his legs. His tail was brown. His wings were brown, marked with black and white and slate. His bill was thick and rather short.

"Who are you?" demanded Peter very bluntly and impolitely.

"I'm Piny the Pine Grosbeak," replied the stranger, seemingly not at all put out by Peter's bluntness.

"Oh," said Peter. "Are you related to Rosebreast the Grosbeak who nested last summer in the Old Orchard?"

"I certainly am," replied Piny. "He is my very own cousin. I've never seen him because he never ventures up where I live and I don't go down where he spends the winter, but all members of the Grosbeak family are cousins."

"Rosebreast is very lovely and I'm very fond of him," said Peter. "We are very good friends."

"Then I know we are going to be good friends," replied Piny. As he said this he turned and Peter noticed that his tail was distinctly forked instead of being square across like that of Welcome Robin. Piny whistled, and almost at once he was joined by another bird who in shape was just like him, but who was dressed in slaty-gray and olive-yellow, instead of the bright red that he himself wore. Piny introduced the newcomer as Mrs. Grosbeak.

"Lovely weather, isn't it?" said she. "I love the snow. I wouldn't feel at home with no snow about. Why, last spring I even built my nest before the snow was gone in the Far North. We certainly hated to leave up there, but food was getting so scarce that we had to. We have just arrived. Can you tell me if there are any cedar-trees or ash-trees or sumacs near here?"

Peter hastened to tell her just where she would find these trees and then rather timidly asked why she wanted to find them.

"Because they hold their berries all winter," replied Mrs. Grosbeak promptly, "and those berries make very good eating. I rather thought there must be some around here. If there are enough of them we certainly shall stay a while."

"I hope you will," replied Peter. "I want to get better acquainted with you. You know, if it were not for you folks who come down from the Far North the Green Forest would be rather a lonely place in winter. There are times when I like to be alone, but I like to feel that there is someone I can call on when I feel lonesome. Did you and Piny come down alone?"

"No, indeed," replied Mrs. Grosbeak. "There is a flock of our relatives not far away. We came down with the Crossbills. All together we made quite a party."

Peter and Jumper stayed a while to gossip with the Grosbeaks. Then Peter bethought him that it was high time for him to return to the dear Old Briar-patch, and bidding his new friends good-by, he started off through the Green Forest, lipperty-lipperty-lip. When he reached the edge of the Green Forest he decided to run over to the weedy field to see if the Snowflakes and the Tree Sparrows and the Horned Larks were there. They were, but almost at once Peter discovered that they had company. Twittering cheerfully as he busily picked seeds out of the top of a weed which stood above the snow, was a bird very little bigger than Chicoree the Goldfinch. But when Peter looked at him he just had to rub his eyes.

"Gracious goodness!" he muttered, "it must be something is wrong with my eyes so that I am seeing red. I've already seen two birds dressed in red and now there's another. It certainly must be my eyes. There's Dotty the Tree Sparrow over there; I hear his voice. I wonder if he will look red."

Peter hopped near enough to get a good look at Dotty and found him dressed just as he should be. That relieved Peter's mind. His eyes were quite as they should be. Then he returned to look at the happy little stranger still busily picking seeds from that weed-top.

The top of his head was bright red. There was no doubt about it. His back was toward Peter at the time and but for that bright red cap Peter certainly would have taken him for one of his friends among the Sparrow family. You see his back was grayish-brown. Peter could think of several Sparrows with backs very much like it. But when he looked closely he saw that just above his tail this little stranger wore a pinkish patch, and that was something no Sparrow of Peter's acquaintance possesses.

Then the lively little stranger turned to face Peter and a pair of bright eyes twinkled mischievously. "Well," said he, "how do you like my appearance? Anything wrong with me? I was taught that it is very impolite to stare at any one. I guess your mother forgot to teach you manners."

Peter paid no attention to what was said but continued to stare. "My, how pretty you are!" he exclaimed.

The little stranger *was* pretty. His breast was *pink*. Below this he was white. The middle of his throat was black and his sides were streaked with reddish-brown. He looked pleased at Peter's exclamation.

"I'm glad you think I'm pretty," said he. "I like pink myself. I like it very much indeed. I suppose you've already seen my friends, Snipper the Crossbill and Piny the Grosbeak."

Peter promptly bobbed his head. "I've just come from making their acquaintance," said he. "By the way you speak, I presume you also are from the Far North. I am just beginning to learn that there are more folks who make their homes in the Far North than I had dreamed of. If you please, I don't believe I know you at all."

"I'm Redpoll," was the prompt response. "I am called that because of my red cap. Yes, indeed, I make my home in the

Far North. There is no place like it. You really ought to run up there and get acquainted with the folks who make their homes there and love it."

Redpoll laughed at his own joke, but Peter didn't see the joke at all. "Is it so very far?" he asked innocently; then added, "I'd dearly love to go."

Redpoll laughed harder than ever. "Yes," said he, "it is. I am afraid you would be a very old and very gray Rabbit by the time you got there. I guess the next thing is for you to make the acquaintance of some of us who get down here once in awhile."

Redpoll called softly and almost at once was joined by another red-capped bird but without the pink breast, and with sides more heavily streaked. "This is Mrs. Redpoll," announced her lively little mate. Then he turned to her and added, "I've just been telling Peter Rabbit that as long as he cannot visit our beautiful Far North he must become acquainted with those of us who come down here in the winter. I'm sure he'll find us very friendly folks."

"I'm sure I shall," said Peter. "If you please, do you live altogether on these weed seeds?"

Redpoll laughed his usual happy laugh. "Hardly, Peter," replied he. "We like the seeds of the birches and the alders, and we eat the seeds of the evergreen trees when we get them. Sometimes we find them in cones Snipper the Crossbill has opened but hasn't picked all the seeds out of. Sometimes he drops some for us. Oh, we always manage to get plenty to eat. There are some of our relatives over there and we must join them. We'll see you again, Peter."

Peter said he hoped they would and then watched them fly over to join their friends. Suddenly, as if a signal had been given, all spread their wings at the same instant and flew up in a birch-tree not far away. All seemed to take wing at precisely the same instant. Up in the birch-tree they sat for a minute or so and then, just as if another signal had been given, all began to pick out the tiny seeds from the birch tassels. No one bird seemed to be first. It was quite like a drill, or as if each had thought of the same thing at the same instant. Peter chuckled over it all the way home. And somehow he felt better for having made the acquaintance of the Redpolls. It was the feeling that everybody so fortunate as to meet them on a gold winter's day is sure to have.

XLV. Peter Sees Two Terrible Feathered Hunters.

While it is true that Peter Rabbit likes winter, it is also true that life is anything but easy for him that season. In the first place he has to travel about a great deal to get sufficient food, and that means that he must run more risks. There isn't a minute of day or night that he is outside of the dear Old Briar-patch when he can afford not to watch and listen for danger. You see, at this season of the year, Reddy Fox often finds it difficult to get a good meal. He is hungry most of the time, and he is forever hunting for Peter Rabbit. With snow on the ground and no leaves on the bushes and young trees, it is not easy for Peter to hide. So, as he travels about, the thought of Reddy Fox is always in his mind.

But there are others whom Peter fears even more, and these wear feathers instead of fur coats. One of these is Terror the Goshawk. Peter is not alone in his fear of Terror. There is not one among his feathered friends who will not shiver at the mention of Terror's name. Peter will not soon forget the day he discovered that Terror had come down from the Far North, and was likely to stay for the rest of the winter. Peter went hungry all the rest of that day.

You see it was this way: Peter had gone over to the Green Forest very early that morning in the hope of getting breakfast in a certain swamp. He was hopping along, lipperty-lipperty-lip, with his thoughts chiefly on that breakfast he hoped to get, but at the same time with ears and eyes alert for possible danger, when a strange feeling swept over him. It was a feeling that great danger was very near, though he saw nothing and heard nothing to indicate it. It was just a feeling, that was all.

Now Peter has learned that the wise thing to do when one has such a feeling as that is to seek safety first and investigate afterwards. At the instant he felt that strange feeling of fear he was passing a certain big, hollow log. Without really knowing why he did it, because, you know, he didn't stop to do any thinking, he dived into that hollow log, and even as he did so there was the sharp swish of great wings. Terror the Goshawk had missed catching Peter by the fraction of a second.

With his heart thumping as if it were trying to pound its way through his ribs, Peter peeped out of that hollow log. Terror had alighted on a tall stump only a few feet away. To Peter in his fright he seemed the biggest bird he ever had seen. Of course he wasn't. Actually he was very near the same size as Redtail the Hawk, whom Peter knew well. He was handsome. There was no denying the fact that he was handsome.

His back was bluish. His head seemed almost black. Over and behind each eye was a white line. Underneath he was beautifully marked with wavy bars of gray and white. On his tail were four dark bands. Yes, he was handsome. But Peter had no thought for his beauty. He could see nothing but the fierceness of the eyes that were fixed on the entrance to that hollow log. Peter shivered as if with a cold chill. He knew that in Terror was no pity or gentleness.

"I hope," thought Peter, "that Mr. and Mrs. Grouse are nowhere about." You see he knew that there is no one that Terror would rather catch than a member of the Grouse family.

Terror did not sit on that stump long. He knew that Peter was not likely to come out in a hurry. Presently he flew away, and Peter suspected from the direction in which he was headed that Terror was going over to visit Farmer Brown's henyard. Of all the members of the Hawk family there is none more bold than Terror the Goshawk. He would not hesitate to seize a hen from almost beneath Farmer Brown's nose. He is well named, for the mere suspicion that he is anywhere about strikes terror to the heart of all the furred and feathered folks. He is so swift of wing that few can escape him, and he has no pity, but kills for the mere love of killing. In this respect he is like Shadow the Weasel. To kill for food is forgiven by the little people of the

Green Forest and the Green Meadows, but to kill needlessly is unpardonable. This is why Terror the Goshawk is universally hated and has not a single friend.

All that day Peter remained hidden in that hollow log. He did not dare put foot outside until the Black Shadows began to creep through the Green Forest. Then he knew that there was nothing more to fear from Terror the Goshawk, for he hunts only by day. Once more Peter's thoughts were chiefly of his stomach, for it was very, very empty.

But it was not intended that Peter should fill his stomach at once. He had gone but a little way when from just ahead of him the silence of the early evening was broken by a terrifying sound—"Whooo-hoo-hoo, whooo-hoo!" It was so sudden and there was in it such a note of fierceness that Peter had all he could do to keep from jumping and running for dear life. But he knew that voice and he knew, too, that safety lay in keeping perfectly still. So with his heart thumping madly, as when he had escaped from Terror that morning, Peter sat as still as if he could not move.

It was the hunting call of Hooty the Great Horned Owl, and it had been intended to frighten some one into jumping and running, or at least into moving ever so little. Peter knew all about that trick of Hooty's. He knew that in all the Green Forest there are no ears so wonderful as those of Hooty the Owl, and that the instant he had uttered that fierce hunting call he had strained those wonderful ears to catch the faintest sound which some startled little sleeper of the night might make. The rustle of a leaf would be enough to bring Hooty to the spot on his great silent wings, and then his fierce yellow eyes, which are made for seeing in the dusk, would find the victim.

So Peter sat still, fearful that the very thumping of his heart might reach those wonderful ears. Again that terrible hunting cry rang out, and again Peter had all he could do to keep from jumping. But he didn't jump, and a few minutes later, as he sat staring at a certain tall, dead stub of a tree, wondering just where Hooty was, the top of that stub seemed to break off, and a great, broad-winged bird flew away soundlessly like a drifting shadow. It was Hooty himself. Sitting perfectly straight on the top of that tall, dead stub he had seemed a part of it. Peter waited some time before he ventured to move. Finally he heard Hooty's hunting call in a distant part of the Green Forest, and knew that it was safe for him to once more think of his empty stomach.

Later in the winter while the snow still lay in the Green Forest, and the ice still bound the Laughing Brook, Peter made a surprising discovery. He was over in a certain lonely part of the Green Forest when he happened to remember that near there was an old nest which had once belonged to Redtail the Hawk. Out of idle curiosity Peter ran over for a look at that old nest. Imagine how surprised he was when just as he came within sight of it, he saw a great bird just settling down on it. Peter's heart jumped right up in his throat. At least that is the way it seemed, for he recognized Mrs. Hooty.

Of course Peter stopped right where he was and took the greatest care not to move or make a sound. Presently Hooty himself appeared and perched in a tree near at hand. Peter has seen Hooty many times before, but always as a great, drifting shadow in the moonlight. Now he could see him clearly. As he sat bolt upright he seemed to be of the same height as Terror the Goshawk, but with a very much bigger body. If Peter had but known it, his appearance of great size was largely due to the fluffy feathers in which Hooty was clothed. Like his small cousin, Spooky the Screech Owl, Hooty seemed to have no neck at all. He looked as if his great head was set directly on his shoulders. From each side of his head two great tufts of feathers stood out like ears or horns. His bill was sharply hooked. He was dressed wholly in reddish-brown with little buff and black markings, and on his throat was a white patch. His legs were feathered, and so were his feet clear to the great claws.

But it was on the great, round, fierce, yellow eyes that Peter kept his own eyes. He had always thought of Hooty as being able to see only in the dusk of evening or on moonlight nights, but somehow he had a feeling that even now in broad daylight Hooty could see perfectly well, and he was quite right.

For a long time Peter sat there without moving. He dared not do anything else. After he had recovered from his first fright he began to wonder what Hooty and Mrs. Hooty were doing at that old nest. His curiosity was aroused. He felt that he simply must find out. By and by Hooty flew away. Very carefully, so as not to attract the attention of Mrs. Hooty, Peter stole back the way he had come.

When he was far enough away to feel reasonably safe, he scampered as fast as ever he could. He wanted to get away from that place, and he wanted to find some one of whom he could ask questions.

Presently he met his cousin, Jumper the Hare, and at once in a most excited manner told him all he had seen.

Jumper listened until Peter was through. "If you'll take my advice," said he, "you'll keep away from that part of the Green Forest, Cousin Peter. From what you tell me it is quite clear to me that the Hooties have begun nesting."

"Nesting!" exclaimed Peter. "Nesting! Why, gentle Mistress Spring will not get here for a month yet!"

"I said *nesting*," retorted Jumper, speaking rather crossly, for you see he did not like to have his word doubted. "Hooty the Great Horned Owl doesn't wait for Mistress Spring. He and Mrs. Hooty believe in getting household cares out of the way early. Along about this time of year they hunt up an old nest of Redtail the Hawk or Blacky the Crow or Chatterer the Red Squirrel, for they do not take the trouble to build a nest themselves. Then Mrs. Hooty lays her eggs while there is still snow and ice. Why their youngsters don't catch their death from cold when they hatch out is more than I can say. But they don't. I'm sorry to hear that the Hooties have a nest here this year. It means a bad time for a lot of little folks in feathers and fur. I certainly shall keep away from that part of the Green Forest, and I advise you to."

Peter said that he certainly should, and then started on for the dear Old Briar-patch to think things over. The discovery that already the nesting season of a new year had begun turned Peter's thoughts towards the coming of sweet Mistress Spring and the return of his many feathered friends who had left for the far-away South so long before. A great longing to hear the voices of Welcome Robin and Winsome Bluebird and Little Friend the Song Sparrow swept over him, and a still greater longing for a bit of friendly gossip with Jenny Wren. In the past year he had learned much about his feathered neighbors, but there were still many things he wanted to know, things which only Jenny Wren could tell him. He was only just beginning to find out that no one knows all there is to know, especially about the birds. And no one ever will.

www.ingramcontent.com/pod-product-compliance
Lightning Source LLC
Chambersburg PA
CBHW031543260326
41914CB00002B/240

9781922634689